AF228483

THE DEVIL and His ADVOCATES

THE DEVIL
AND HIS
ADVOCATES

ERIK BUTLER

REAKTION BOOKS

Published by Reaktion Books Ltd
Unit 32, Waterside
44–48 Wharf Road
London N1 7UX, UK
www.reaktionbooks.co.uk

First published 2021
Copyright © Erik Butler 2021

Printed and bound in Great Britain by
TJ Books Ltd, Padstow, Cornwall

A catalogue record for this book is available from the British Library

ISBN 978 1 78914 373 7

Contents

Two interpreters of Scripture: Michael Pacher, *The Devil Presenting St Augustine with the Book of Vices*, c. 1480, oil on panel; detail from the outside panel of the *Altarpiece of the Church Fathers* (*Kirchenväteraltar*).

Introduction: Thank God for the Devil!

'*Satan* has something of religion in him', Daniel Defoe observes in *The Political History of the Devil* (1726).[1] This work, which is old but not dated, defends the Adversary against imputations of intrigue as practised by 'our old Friend *Matchiavel*' and other 'sons of *Adam*'.

> The *Devil's history* is not so hard to come at, as it seems to be; his original and the first rise of his family is upon record; and as for his conduct, he has acted indeed in the dark, as to method in many things; but *in general*, as cunning as he is, he . . . has not shewn himself a politician at all.[2]

Satan does not act faithlessly to achieve earthly ends. Only people do that. The Devil '*is a believer*' and he '*fears God*'.[3] These qualities set him apart from many, if not most, mortal servants of the Lord.

In the same spirit as Defoe's vindication of the Devil, the study at hand proposes the forensic history of a wrongly maligned figure. Instead of presenting himself in a shower of fire and brimstone, Satan often plays the part of a lawyer. He musters evidence, makes arguments and ultimately wins or loses the case before the one – and only – Divine Judge. If Satan has a bad reputation, it's because he has a thankless job.

For about four hundred years, the Roman Catholic Church appointed a theologian called the *promotor fidei* – in English, 'promoter of the faith' – to oversee the process of beatification and canonization. Informally, the *promotor fidei* went by the name of *advocatus diaboli*, or 'Devil's advocate'. A sceptic by vocation, this officer weighed proof, examined witnesses and offered alternative explanations for supposed wonders. Whenever the Church was thinking about conferring sainthood on a person, limiting factors entered the equation; other points of view had to be considered. A recent study on the psychology of influence summarizes the matter with a felicitous understatement: 'the Church instituted this role as insurance against groupthink . . . Not everyone . . . should be sainted.'[4] Sometimes the minority position is right.

The Devil stands in the service of truth. The following pages seek to explain his activities in order to check the usual rush to judgement. Questions of good and evil arise, but they represent items of secondary importance. Instead, attention falls on arguments – whether explicit, as in theological debate, or implicit, as in literary discourse – that make the case for apparent wrongs, moral or otherwise. The Deity's designs are famously obscure; the Devil serves to bring them to fruition in roundabout fashion.

Our discussion remains anchored in the Bible, where the popular image of Satan as an unbridled force of wickedness finds no support. In both Testaments, the Devil is surprisingly modest. He makes few appearances and, without a bow, vanishes from the stage when his work is done. *The Devil and His Advocates* explores representations of the Adversary up to the present day in light of the scriptural standard. Counter to widespread prejudice, he is not the eternal 'bad guy'.

Chapter One, 'The Case for the Prosecution', establishes the frame of argument by examining Jewish and Christian sources. The Book of Job is the sole place in the Tanakh, or Hebrew Bible, where Satan has any real stature. He is one of the 'sons of God'. When Satan expresses doubt about Job's virtue, God gives him leave to determine whether the righteous man will remain loyal under terrible conditions. Satan exercises rigour, but within the bounds of divine instruction. The New Testament seems to flesh out Satan and endow him with a will of his own. However, closer inspection reveals that when he tempts – or, more accurately, makes trial of – Jesus, he is acting in line with his long-standing role as a prosecutor. Once more, he loses his case. The Adversary may be unpleasantly exacting, but no more so than a policeman, bailiff or other representative of authority.

Chapter Two, 'Satan and Salvation', explores the part the Adversary plays in the Book of Revelation. Although he might appear to work at cross-purposes with God, his presence is welcome. This late and controversial addition to the Bible rejoices at the imminent fall of pagan civilization. As war raged between Romans and Jews, monotheists embraced a bellicose stance towards those who refused to acknowledge the Lord. The Book of Revelation does not view Satan as an enemy: he is a fearsome ally in the coming judgement of humankind, which God has willed and His followers should embrace.

Chapter Three, 'The Adversary at Home and Abroad', begins by examining the shape that early theologians gave the 'other world' as a place of punishment and reward – a conception indebted to pagan cosmology and myth. The centrepiece is Dante

Alighieri's *Divine Comedy*. Like the scholastic philosophy of his day, Dante's poem maps out a metaphysical reality directly connected to the physical universe; indeed, it is populated by historical figures the author knew well. Satan sits deep in darkness and cold, embodying forces that draw human beings away from life and light. The picture conforms to biblical logic: Satan represents the negative index of truth. Those who fail the tests posed by earthly existence face 'living death' now and, even worse, 'dead life' in the hereafter. Self-destructively playful devils in Dante's poem and contemporary works are exceptions that prove the rule – reminders that God permits levity but refuses the last laugh to sinners who go too far.

Chapter Four, 'Doubt, Dissent and the Devil', turns to schisms in the Church and the trials they entailed. The old word for belief at variance with official doctrine is 'heresy', and orthodoxy had long sought to silence dissenting voices. In the Age of Reformation, rival versions of Christianity that differed on everything else shared two fundamental convictions: 1) God is great, and 2) the opponents of true religion have chosen to side with Satan. Perfect agreement on matters of principle led Christians to kill each other mercilessly – to say nothing of people who lacked sufficient numbers or organization for self-defence (such as 'witches'). Christopher Marlowe's *Doctor Faustus* is discussed alongside Robert Burton's *Anatomy of Melancholy*, German chapbooks, Shakespearean devilry and the French Wars of Religion. The Devil thrives when confessional sophistry is more compelling than the Gospel's simple eloquence.

Chapter Five, 'The Devil's Party', looks at post-Reformation representations of Satan. In John Milton's *Paradise Lost*, the former 'Angel of Light' appears as an orator and statesman in his own sovereign domain. Outside this sphere, in the Garden of Eden, he bumbles as he tries to persuade Adam and Eve to file suit against the Lord. No matter how poorly he exercises his profession, Satan remains a lawyer, by turns a legislator and a litigator. Goethe's *Faust* shows the Devil as a cynical member of the bar. Mephistopheles maintains that nothing any mortal does can amount to anything. He proves as much by allowing the play's hero to indulge his every whim; Faust does not manage even to build castles in the sky. Finally, our attention turns to how Romantic poetry displays a satanic bent by toying with social and moral convention. Humanity's 'enemy' now presents himself as a 'friend'. When Satan adopts the role of an intimate, he is playing a confidence game to expose disloyalty.

Chapter Six, 'Sick, Sick, Sick', digs deeper into the literary cult of Satan in the period from the French Revolution to the First World War. Rationalism, empiricism and positivist theory conjured up the Devil as powerfully as any old-fashioned superstition. Our focus is Catholic writers who disbelieved schemes of improvement and hymned Satan's regime for body and soul. The works of Jules-Amédée Barbey d'Aurevilly, Charles Baudelaire, Léon Bloy and Joris-Karl Huysmans are legal briefs against clemency for humankind. In an age that promised to heal the world by instituting new and better conditions of life, the reactionary vanguard prized pathology like a holy relic and turned to the Devil to find the Lord.

To put the abiding role of Satan into relief, Chapter Seven, 'The Godawful Truth', surveys works that would discard inherited dogma in favour of new, secular revelation. Although a man of no faith, Sigmund Freud acknowledged that religious instincts persist as urgently as sexual drives and unconscious forces eclipse rational understanding; given the human inability to control such impulses, they might as well be supernatural. Authors as varied as Fyodor Dostoevsky, William Butler Yeats, Oskar Panizza and Gottfried Benn confirm Freud's diagnosis. Most people cannot handle a 'godless' world – especially without the Devil there to take some of the heat.

Chapter Eight, 'A Satanic Symphony', adds music to the equation. After analysing pious hymns in ancient, medieval and early modern cultures, we turn to Thomas Mann's *Doctor Faustus* for a discussion that reaches from Germany, twentieth-century European history and classical music to globalism, geopolitics and rock 'n' roll. Mann's novel about a composer soaring and crashing on the wings of song offers an allegory for culture torn between opposites: nationalism and socialism, tribalism and brotherhood, atavism and advancement. Satan is our contemporary, whether he really exists or not.

A brief coda draws up the balance. It cannot be said often or strongly enough: according to biblical logic, Satan represents a secondary instance of power, subordinate to the Lord. If there's a problem, take it up with *Him*. Satan gets stuck with all the dirty work and all the blame, even though he contributes to the fulfilment of God's plans. May the poor Devil finally get his due.

ONE

The Case for the Prosecution

'Satan' is not a name in the Hebrew Bible, or Tanakh. *Ha-satan* means 'the opponent' or 'the accuser'. With a definite article, the word occurs in only two books, Job and Zechariah. Elsewhere, *satan* appears just ten times and means someone who gets in the way of someone else (and not necessarily with ill intent). It is translation that suggests personhood where the source uses a generic phrasing: 'the satan' or 'a satan' turns into Satan. The same occurs when the New Testament, which was written in Greek, is put into English or another modern language. Words designating a function or role come to sound as if they referred to a being of cosmic eminence with an independent will. Viewing the satan as a kind of supervillain on the same transcendental plane as God – *Satan*, writ large – is wrong according to both the Hebrew and Christian Bibles.

The popular mind has long imagined an embodiment of evil set on foiling Providence; a certain degree of ambivalence and illusion beseems the subject. But by identifying a diabolical *function*, a distinct and limited role conforming to divine will, we can dispel any number of misconceptions and bring a clearer picture into view.

The Adversary serves as a touchstone for truth. The question of righteous human conduct cannot be posed, much less answered, without considering obstructions and complications. The satan/ Satan may be more of a bit player than is usually assumed – indeed, not really a 'character' at all – but his presence is vital if mortals are to understand what God asks of them and where to steer their steps.

Job's Innocence

The Book of Job tells the story of a model father and community leader in the land of Uz, an individual who, as the King James Version puts it, 'was perfect and upright . . . feared God, and eschewed evil' (1:1).[1] Blessed with possessions and progeny, Job is esteemed 'the greatest of all the men' (1:3) by his fellows. He 'continually' (1:5) offers sacrifices to God, lest sins by members of his household warrant retribution from the Lord. His good fortune does not last.

> Now there was a day when the sons of God came to present themselves before the Lord, and Satan came also among them. And the Lord said unto Satan, 'Whence comest thou?' Then Satan answered the Lord, and said, 'From going to and fro in the earth, and from walking up and down in it.' And the Lord said unto Satan, 'Hast thou considered my servant Job, that there is none like him in the earth, a perfect and an upright man, one that feareth God, and escheweth evil?' Then Satan answered the Lord, and said, 'Doth Job fear God for nought? Hast not thou made an hedge about him, and about his house, and about all that he hath on every side? Thou hast blessed the work of his hands, and his substance is increased in the land. But put forth thine hand now, and

touch all that he hath, and he will curse thee to thy face.' And the Lord said unto Satan, 'Behold, all that he hath is in thy power; only upon himself put not forth thine hand.' So Satan went forth from the presence of the Lord (1:6–12).

And so Job's afflictions begin. First he loses his livestock, then his servants and finally his children. Job mourns, but 'in all this, [he] sinned not, nor charged God foolishly' (1: 2). Satan is confounded. Again he approaches God and obtains authorization to see how the righteous man will comport himself under duress. Job is covered with 'boils from the sole of his foot unto his crown' (2:7). Although he comes to rue the day of his birth, Job never curses God. The ordeal is the pious mortal's glory. At long last, after the most grievous suffering a man can endure, Job is rewarded for his forbearance and faith with 'twice as much as he had before' (42:10).

A quick glance at the text suggests that the sworn enemy of humankind has induced God to allow him to subject His faithful servant to horrible torture and trial. This is partially accurate, yet it is not the whole truth. For one, as we remarked at the outset, translation changes the sense of the Hebrew text by making *ha-satan* a proper noun. In the original, the word is a title – 'the satan'. What's more, this figure numbers among the 'sons of God'– that is, he belongs to an elect host. The satan 'goes to and fro' in the created world. Such 'walking up and down' indicates his marginal status, yet no stigma is attached to his position, nor does it mean that he actually stands outside God's law. On the contrary: inasmuch as he comes 'before the Lord' to file regular reports, the satan belongs to a kind of itinerant police force; he patrols the kingdom and makes sure that order prevails.[2] Nothing in the

Satan makes the case for testing Job and breaking his 'arrogant spirit': Philip Galle, after Maarten van Heemskerck, 'The Sons of God, Satan amongst Them, Present Themselves before Him', 1563, engraving from the series of eight plates *The Story of Job* (*Geschiedenis van Job*).

Book of Job implies that the satan entertains hostile relations with the ruler of the cosmos.

The satan is more an observer than an agent. No mention is made of his inherent destructiveness, and he demonstrates no malice. He reports for duty, shares what he has seen and, when asked, expresses doubt that God's favourite would conduct himself so nobly under other circumstances. 'Satan' has few traits to set him apart from other 'sons of God'. In contrast to the Lord – who is unknown, unknowable and commands awe – the satan does not evoke depth; he appears only in silhouette.

The scenes of Job's affliction make no mention of the satan, either. No fiend with a pitchfork or boiling oil comes to torment and taunt the righteous man. In fact, nothing discernibly super-natural (much less diabolical) takes place: the misfortunes that befall Job might strike any mortal.

And there was a day when his sons and his daughters were eating and drinking wine in their eldest brother's house. And there came a messenger unto Job, and said, 'The oxen were plowing, and the asses feeding beside them. And the Sabeans fell upon them, and took them away; yea, they have slain the servants with the edge of the sword; and I only am escaped alone to tell thee.' While he was yet speaking, there came also another, and said, 'The fire of God is fallen from heaven, and hath burned up the sheep, and the servants, and consumed them; and I only am escaped alone to tell thee.' While he was yet speaking, there came also another, and said, 'The Chaldeans made out three bands, and fell upon the camels, and have carried them away, yea, and slain the servants with the edge of the sword; and I only am escaped alone to tell thee.' While he was yet speaking, there came also another, and said, 'Thy sons and thy daughters were eating and drinking wine in their eldest brother's house. And, behold, there came a great wind from the wilderness, and smote the four corners of the house, and it fell upon the young men, and they are dead; and I only am escaped alone to tell thee' (1:13–19).

First, the Sabeans and Chaldeans raid Job's homestead. Then, 'a great wind from the wilderness' brings further ruin. The rapid arrival of messengers and their formulaic speech ('I only am escaped alone') heighten emotional impact but do not point to an otherworldly power; blows that might come over the course of a lifetime strike in an instant. Although one of the messengers reports that the 'fire of God is fallen from heaven', the words should not necessarily be taken literally; the phrase can mean lightning.[3] At any rate, it is 'fire of God', not 'fire of Satan'. Inasmuch as events are not described directly, but as if they were taking place onstage, they are more mythical than factual – stylized for effect. This does not mean they are untrue, only that, as the subsequent narrative underscores, the Deity's will lies beyond human grasp. Perhaps the satan has simply let things run their course; after all, he has been instructed *not* to 'put . . . forth [his] hand'. The catastrophe Job suffers is certain, but its cause is not. What matters is the man's conduct when faced with adversity.

In order to appreciate biblical wisdom, it is important to avoid viewing events merely as signs of Satan's cruelty and/or God's (temporary) indifference.[4] All the hardships that Job experiences come from the physical universe; human beings either create or compound them. The righteous sufferer's worst torment occurs when his wife and friends enjoin him to acknowledge that he must have done something wrong to warrant misfortune. People who are not as 'perfect and upright' as Job himself would add to his grief by insisting that he deserves punishment.

> Then said his wife unto him, 'Dost thou still retain thine integrity? Curse God, and die.' But he said unto her, 'Thou speakest as one of the foolish women speaketh. What? shall

we receive good at the hand of God, and shall we not receive evil?' (2:9–10).

This exchange illustrates the difference between Job and his spouse, who possess diametrically opposed views of humankind's relation to the Deity. Job is a loyal servant. His wife is not. He may stand above other mortals, yet he occupies a station immeasurably inferior to God (and His court). Job is worthy of whatever advantages he has enjoyed, but only because of generosity from on high. At the same time, his dignified forbearance places him above human judgement – which is precisely what his wife fails to understand. Her words exemplify the incomprehension of ordinary people when disaster strikes. It is logical, if also mistaken, in theological terms, to assume that fortune signifies divine favour and misfortune disfavour. The discourses of Job's friends follow the same specious reasoning.[5]

Efforts to make Job admit guilt represent magical thinking, which seeks an agent behind every event, a cause behind every effect. A superstitious mindset like this cannot accept that things may happen that no act of sacrifice can reverse. Without recognizing as much, Job's wife and friends urge him to offer the ultimate reparation by cursing God – that is, to invite catastrophe openly, which would justify everything that has befallen him after the fact. Were their attempts successful, the poor man would consent to expulsion from the collective, if not to violent elimination at its hands.

Job will not commit any wrong. He retains in adversity the nobility of spirit that he displayed when conditions favoured him. Like a good son, Job acknowledges the authority of the divine Father, even though he is perplexed and miserable the whole time. His steadfastness represents a theological position, not just a personal attitude.

'Satan' is simply 'the satan' in the Tanakh, a quasi-anonymous functionary whose role is to drive home a profound lesson. The blows that hammer Job are in line with disasters that can occur when nature (which includes human nature) follows its normal course. Great winds of destruction arise often enough, and the earth teems with people who act like the Sabeans and Chaldeans (or, for that matter, like Job's wife and friends). In no way does the satan seek to promote evil for evil's sake. Instead, he visits trials upon God's model servant in order to test his mettle. In the process it becomes clear what 'good' and 'evil' really mean.

The Book of Job exposes a disquieting truth about human beings. People will seek someone to blame when calamity afflicts their community, and they deem bad luck the manifestation of supernatural will: payback for wrongs committed. Worse still, they aggravate the ills at hand with wickedness of their own by accusing and persecuting the abject and unfortunate, even – and especially – when the latter are innocent. Such perversity follows the primitive need to reduce cosmic occurrences to human terms. A wiser view holds that God has no obligation to make anything comprehensible to beings with finite moral and intellectual faculties.[6] The events that constitute the vast and complex world do not follow the logic of mortal minds or the wishes of the human heart. Men and women are inclined to find fault with others and blame them for what they themselves fail to understand; in so doing, they inflict further wrongs. Error is their native element, rampant with hypocritical cruelty.

After the first two chapters, Satan/the satan vanishes from the Book of Job. He scarcely appears again in the rest of the Old

Testament, which presents a veritable litany of misdeeds that people perform all on their own: incest, murder, idolatry, betrayal and so on. This relatively low-level functionary is not the source of trouble. He ventures a hypothesis, receives authorization to test it and finds out that he is wrong. Had Job's woes beset anybody else in the land of Uz (or the rest of the globe), the results might have been very different. Even though Job is rewarded for forbearance and piety, the ending does not affirm that a similar outcome will occur for others.

Earthly Conflict and Heavenly Revolt

Popular beliefs and practices never follow official precepts alone. The 'People of the Book' are no exception. Judaism developed through encounters with neighbouring tribes, and it incorporated elements of foreign belief systems – the gods, spirits and demons of others.[7] Over and over, Moses chastises those he leads for lapsing into pagan worship. Biblical kings and priests do not always observe the rules, and the prophets denounce their people's shortcomings with savagery that would qualify as hate-speech in the modern world.[8] The diaspora brought about further changes, which have made the religion what it is today.

Now as then, there are multiple Judaisms. The Jews existed as a people and a religious community for centuries before the Bible received definitive form. What historians call the 'intertestamental period' – roughly four hundred years, extending from the last of the Jewish prophets, Malachi (*c.* 420 BCE), to the time of John the Baptist – witnessed the proliferation of writings that were deemed holy by sizeable groups but did not become canonical. To some extent, orthodoxy depends on a fiction of identity that never was.

In a wide-ranging study of comparative mythology, Neil Forsyth has argued that the 'combat myth' accounts for the genesis of Satan, 'the Old Enemy'.[9] The most elementary operation of human thought is to draw dividing lines among the welter of physical and intellectual phenomena in order to arrive at discrete, manageable units of cognition. The distinction between self and other is as basic as the difference between day and night. 'Us' and 'them' come to stand allied with forces working towards order and dissolution, or, in metaphysical terms, good and evil. Points of indeterminacy, confusion and conflict count as intrusions of the alien into the domestic sphere. The result is a scene of attack and defence, renewed time and again.

Forsyth makes an excellent point in stressing the core contradiction that religion seeks to master. All the same, it is important to connect representations to *realia*. Elaine Pagels adds the necessary clarity by showing how the Adversary gained substance when Jews quarrelled with their brethren about their accommodation of, and assimilation to, Gentile culture. Particularly during the Maccabean revolts (167–160 BCE) against the Seleucid Empire, Jewish militants 'began increasingly to invoke the *satan*' when speaking of rivals; in the process, an 'unpleasant figure' assumed 'far grander' dimensions and 'far more malevolent' qualities.[10]

The satanic epithet did not apply to enemies from without so much as to members of the community who had made an easy peace with foreign culture or, worse still, embraced it. In Pagels's words:

Contending less against 'the nations' than against other Jews, [sectarians] denounce their opponents as apostate and accuse them of having been seduced by [a] power . . . they call by many names – Satan, Beelzebub, Semihazah, Azazel, Belial, Prince of Darkness.[11]

Such invective amounts to Deuteronomic curses heaped on parties who would abandon their own people and God. As terms of abuse that echo unwelcome foreignness, 'Beelzebub', 'Semihazah' and the like are anti-names, relegating those they strike to abjection. But an insult is a tacit recognition of power. And so, if only as an effect of language hardened in the forge of internecine battle, Satan emerged as the wicked counterpart to the Lord.

In this framework, Pagels continues, biblical texts could be read for signs of 'cosmic war' between God's loyal servants and those beholden to His enemy, which had been raging since the dawn of time.[12] The tale of the Garden of Eden already offers evidence of an entity bent on the ruin of the created world and the beings made in God's image.

Originally, it seems, the ill-famed serpent was a trickster figure – a type known to all the world's cultures.[13] The crafty reptile succeeds at making Adam and Eve deviate from the straight and narrow, for which it is condemned to crawl on its belly – hating, and hated by, humankind. On its own, the tale teaches the perils of being too clever for one's own good. Like the myth of Prometheus in Greek tradition,[14] it explains why mortals must work the earth to survive; equally, it accounts for the subordinate station of women and the difficulties of gender relations and reproduction. 'The satan' is not part of this picture.[15]

The notion of cosmic war transferred events to a higher plane of abstraction and import. *Adam* means 'human being' or 'humanity' in Hebrew, and *Eve* evokes 'breath' and 'life' – the world's inhabitants in general.[16] Interpreted along allegorical lines, the animal that convinced the archetypal human pair to defy the Deity represents much more, too. No longer simply a trickster, the serpent came to be associated with the folkloric conception of Satan, the faithless enemy who undoes life and religion from within. Inasmuch as mutual obligations and care among human beings are divinely willed, the diabolical serpent would thwart the Creator Himself. In other words, the culturally and politically conflicted atmosphere of the intertestamental period favoured the (re)emergence of combat mythology with an Antagonist practically on a par with God.

The prism of intertestamental culture also explains how Satan earned one of the more puzzling – and enduring – titles applied to him. 'Lucifer', or 'light-bearer' (like the Hebrew word it translates, *helel*), derives from Isaiah. When the ancient prophet speaks of the plunge of the 'shining one' into 'the depths of the pit' (14:12–15), he is referring to one of the many human enemies against whom his people has warred.[17] A generic epithet, 'Lucifer' designates an earthly sovereign; like all kings, he shines as a beacon for his subjects to follow. Having lost in battle, the proud ruler now lies humbled. The biblical text says nothing more than this, but yet again, the words have a different resonance when interpreted in terms of cosmic warfare. Made into a proper noun, 'Lucifer' reads as another name for the eternal Adversary – and a particularly revealing one, too, insofar as it acknowledges the uncanny brightness beaming from what should by rights shed no light at all.

The body of so-called apocryphal or pseudepigraphal literature of the intertestamental period, which is sprawling and difficult to survey, includes many tales that exercised immense influence in their time and shape religious conceptions even now.[18] Chief among them is the legend so well known to posterity that one might almost be forgiven for thinking it part of the Hebrew Bible: how rebel angels mutinied against God and were struck down for their presumption.[19] Indeed, after much debate, echoes made it into the New Testament in the enigmatic and controversial Book of Revelation (which we will discuss in the next chapter).[20]

Pseudepigraphal comes from the Greek for 'falsely attributed'. In both Jewish and Gentile cultures, a standard way to bolster claims was to ascribe them to a figure of established antiquity and authority. Among the many texts of this kind, the so-called *Book of Enoch* warrants particular notice. According to the Bible, Noah's great-grandfather still 'walked with God' (Genesis 5:22). Occupying a position between the generations before the Flood and those afterward, Enoch has come to stand for wisdom in rabbinical Judaism, the guardian of divine secrets. The roots of this tradition lie in the intertestamental period.[21]

The *Book of the Watchers*, which comprises part of the *Book of Enoch*, presents an alternative view of the higher reality governing the world. Enoch describes his journeys over the earth and through the realm of the dead (*Sheol*). His narrative yields a picture mapped out along the lines of west, east, north and south where physical and metaphysical geography fuse into one. Past, present and future lie open before him.

From a supernal perspective, the seer or guardian reveals events and sacred truths that the Bible omits or does not explain. These include the backstory to an obscure passage in Genesis that immediately precedes the Deity's decision to scrap life on earth, with the exception of Noah and the passengers on the ark:

And it came to pass, when men began to multiply . . . and daughters were born unto them, that the sons of God saw the daughters of men that they were fair; and they took them wives of all which they chose . . . There were giants in the earth in those days; and also after that, when the sons of God came in unto the daughters of men, and they bare children to them, the same became mighty men which were of old, men of renown (6:1–4).

'Giants' is a questionable rendering; the word comes from Graeco-Latin mythology and names a fearsome brood vanquished by the Olympian gods. Etymologically, it is related to 'earth'.[22] The Hebrew is *nephilim*, which connects with the verb 'to fall'. But however one translates the term, 'sons of God' and 'daughters of men' brought forth a race whose existence violated appointed bounds. 'Mighty' and 'renown' are not inherently positive qualifications. Illegitimate intercourse produced 'warriors' whose violence earned them 'infamy'.

According to the Bible, the tribe born of angels and mortal women should be extinct. The *Book of the Watchers* suggests that the offspring of celestial rebels and human beings – bastard entities embodying a second, perverse Creation – are still working destruction. As Pagels observes, the story of miscegenation has a bearing on pagans claiming descent from the gods. More importantly, it expresses 'a pious people's contempt for a specific group of Jewish enemies', namely 'priests who . . . violate their divinely given status and responsibility' by contracting 'marriages with outsiders'.[23]

Among other things, then, the *Book of the Watchers* is political propaganda. Violating the law of pure descent amounts to warfare against one's brethren. Mutiny in mythical time parallels the situation among mortals 'here and now', when impious foreigners and, worse still, 'bad Jews' threaten the identity and cohesion of the people destined to serve the Lord.

In sum, around the time the historical Jesus walked among men, two conceptions of the Adversary existed. The first was 'the satan', the biblical officer of God who prosecuted potential wrong-doers. The second, 'Satan', represented a less sophisticated set of ideas, incarnating forces of evil and destruction. The former worked in divine service. The latter did not. Like other function-aries of the heavenly court, the lower-case satan enjoyed a certain measure of independence, yet he deferred to authority. This son of God was an agent of discipline and order; even if he showed excessive zeal, he handed cases over to the Lord. The second – upper-case Satan – had many names, and just as many ways of exercising power. Provoking civil strife and defying authority, he is the Devil of later, non-Jewish popular tradition, too, the eternal malcontent contriving misdeeds over and over again, especially through agents who do not qualify as fully human.

Christ's Guilt

It might seem that Satan plays a central role in the New Testament – that now he is a full-blown personality and power in his own right. Certainly, he shows up more often than in the Hebrew Bible. Satan appears in the Gospels, and reference is made to him in the Acts of the Apostles and the Epistles. Yet the Adversary does not display the traits most familiar to later times. In spite of a heightened presence, he remains a cipher and stands in service to the Lord. He is still a 'son of God' – in other words, 'the satan'. The same holds even for the Book of Revelation.

The texts comprising the New Testament were written at different points, but in each case at least a generation after Jesus had died.[24] Their authors did not seek to report historical events in a modern sense. Instead, they wished to proclaim an updated code of belief and conduct for the Chosen People. But why should such bold claims be trusted? In conformity with his role in the Book of Job, Satan – in fact, the satan – makes trial of an extraordinary individual. The outcome affirms the righteousness and dignity of the accused.

Judaism was – and is – sustained by ritual observance that seeks to preserve favourable relations with the Deity. At the same time, and with varying levels of emphasis, the religion has always promised that one day the faithful will be freed from the hardships they face. *Christos* is the Greek word for messiah (*mashiach*), 'the anointed one', who will bring this about. Thus Matthew (1:1–17) and Luke (3:23–38) trace the ancestry of the man in whom they have placed their faith back to David, the exemplary king of Israel. Despite his humble birth in a manger, Jesus has the pedigree required of a leader. His story proves all the more wondrous for having started under ignoble circumstances.

Matthew makes the miraculous beginnings of Jesus' story retell the history of Israel as a whole. Moses, who gave the Jews the laws making them a people with an eternal destiny, is found among the reeds of the Nile; only later does his inborn greatness manifest itself to others, when he delivers his followers from Pharaoh. Likewise, the child who is the man who is the Messiah occupies an outsider position. Jesus, the renewer of the faith, embodies the same holy purpose on a larger scale. The difference is that he wants to free his people from unjust *Jewish* rule. In the Old Testament Moses narrowly escapes the slaughter ordered by a foreign king. The New Testament reports the same wonder, but now the villain is no outsider. That is why Matthew describes Herod's attempt to kill the male children of his subjects. The issue concerns the legitimacy of tradition: on one side stands a bad king who symbolizes how alienated Judaism has grown from its origins, and on the other 'a child is born' who will accomplish great things by leading his brethren back to true religion.

From an untutored standpoint, or following the fancies of a later age, it would make sense for Satan to take the stage when Herod orders the massacre of his own people's sons. However, he makes no appearance. The Hebrew Bible does not portray Satan as a destroyer, and the Gospels do not either. The New Testament presents him as he was at the time of Job: an accuser and prosecuting official. In this capacity, he is distinct from Herod and the Roman overlords with whom the imposturous king of Judea has allied himself.

There are three versions of how Satan – the satan, that is – approaches Jesus. Mark, whose account is the oldest, states simply, 'he was . . . in the wilderness forty days, tempted of Satan; and was with the wild beasts; and the angels ministered unto him' (1:13). The backdrop of the encounter is significant. The meeting immediately follows Jesus' baptism. John the Baptist, who performs the rite, has 'prepare[d] . . . the way of the Lord' (1:3) by preaching in the desert; 'clothed with camel's hair, and with a girdle of skin about his loins', he has survived on 'locusts and wild honey' (1:6). Jesus follows in his footsteps, yet he is 'mightier' (1:7) and therefore destined for worse affliction before ultimate triumph. The desolation of his retreat evokes the hardships endured by the ancient Israelites. The forty days that have elapsed when Satan comes to Jesus recall the forty years his ancestors spent lost and wandering.

When Jesus prevails against the Adversary, he delivers himself and all who would go with him from the toils that made the generation of Moses expire before reaching the Promised Land.

Matthew and Luke, who probably relied on the same source, present more detailed accounts. In substance, they are much the same, but the added detail confirms that Satan/the satan – here called 'the Devil' (*ho diabolos*) – is playing his assigned part in a greater drama. Matthew writes:

> Then was Jesus led up of the Spirit into the wilderness to be tempted of the Devil. And . . . [he] fasted forty days and forty nights . . . And when the tempter came to him, he said, 'If thou be the Son of God, command that these stones be made bread.' But he answered and said, 'It is written, Man shall not live by bread alone, but by every word that proceedeth out of the mouth of God.' Then the Devil taketh him up into the holy city, and setteth him on a pinnacle of the temple, And saith unto him, 'If thou be the Son of God, cast thyself down: for it is written, He shall give his angels charge concerning thee: and in their hands they shall bear thee up . . .' Jesus said unto him, 'It is written again, Thou shalt not tempt the Lord thy God.' Again, the Devil taketh him up into an exceeding high mountain, and sheweth him all the kingdoms of the world, and the glory of them; And saith unto him, 'All these things will I give thee, if thou wilt fall down and worship me.' Then saith Jesus unto him, 'Get thee hence, Satan: for it is written, Thou shalt worship the Lord thy God, and him only shalt thou serve.' Then the Devil leaveth him (4:1–11).

Dirk Vellert, *Christ Tempted by the Devil*, 1525,
etching and engraving.

It is 'the Spirit' that conducts Jesus 'to be tempted'. If 'the Devil' confronts him, this occurs because a higher power has willed it. The word for 'tempted' (*peirasthēnai*) may also be translated as 'tested', and the same holds for related vocabulary. Jesus, like Job before him, is subjected to trial so that his holy status may be proven and stand as fact.

The verification process unfolds in three stages. First, the putative messiah must show himself superior to the desires – indeed, the needs (given his long fasting) – of the flesh. Then, he must not renounce reason by mistaking the letter of the law for its actual meaning, which is spiritual. Jesus refuses to cast himself down from the heights simply because 'it is written' that 'angels … shall bear thee up'. Versed in Scripture, Jesus cites a counter-argument. He forgoes the opportunity to perform tricks simply because he has been challenged to do so; the wonders he works always benefit others. The last part of the ordeal involves rejecting the enticements of earthly might and fame: 'all the kingdoms of the world and the glory of them'.

Ho diabolos means 'slanderer' in Greek. The Devil comes at the appointed time and does his job, but he instigates nothing. Moreover, he leaves once he has performed his task. From a modern, secular perspective, the tests that he administers gauge psychological states – moments of doubt and self-interrogation on the part of the patient about personal fitness to complete a monumental task. *Ho diabolos* might be understood as a mocking voice that comes from within – an impulse psychoanalysts would locate in the unconscious mind. There is no reason to picture an embodied, personified force that comes to Jesus and confronts him. The delirious scene confirms the latter's self-discipline at a moment of tribulation.

Like the Tanakh, the New Testament provides no physical description of the satan/Satan. The Adversary displays no wings, horns, tail or other outward sign of who and what he is. He appears through language alone, speaking words intended to confound Jesus and trip him up. As such, he does not represent a supernatural agent so much as he mirrors Pharisees and other opponents who would do the same – the 'generation of vipers' (Matthew 3:7) with whom Jesus quarrels from the start. As Pagels puts it: 'Satan [is] a caricature of a scribe, a debater skilled in verbal challenge and adept in quoting the Scriptures for diabolical purposes, who repeatedly tests Jesus's divine authority.'[25] The storied 'temptation of Christ' is not a showdown between good and evil so much as a rabbinical disputation. Satan tries to make Jesus incriminate himself, which would invalidate all that he has said to his co-religionists. By withstanding the challenges, Jesus demonstrates the worthiness of his person and cause.

The Pharisees may 'say good things', but they are 'evil' (Matthew 12:34). Pagels interprets this statement, and others like it, to mean that 'political success and power' – which the Pharisees and other representatives of the status quo enjoyed by foreign dispensation – 'evince a pact with the devil.'[26] The Romans are pagans, and so all Jews who derive benefit from making peace with them must be enemies of their own people; their self-serving words amount to hypocrisy and cant. That said, it is misleading to speak of a pact with the Devil, insofar as it implies that Satan holds dominion over the world. Although certain passages seem to say as much (such as 2 Corinthians 4:4 and John 12:31), it is clear, in context, that they refer to the prevailing mood among unbelievers, who persist in denying Jesus and his message. Jesus is taking on parties whose prominent social status would have counted as 'marks of divine favor' to traditionally minded contemporaries.[27] Their world is 'diabolical' insofar as it rests upon slander and ill will.

As a rule, prophets strike the people of their day as noisome; if they didn't, they probably would have no real news. In the interest of historical impartiality, if nothing else, it is worth considering the position of established Jewish interests. Jesus was hardly the sole holy man to present bold claims during the tumultuous inter-testamental period, when radicals of many stripes pulled at the fabric of tradition.[28] The texts that constitute the Christian canon were written in the aftermath – and, in the case of Mark, perhaps during – the First Jewish War (66–70 CE), when Rome asserted its dominance over its client-state in Palestine and destroyed any Jewish pretence to self-rule. Jesus' undermining of Judaism as practised by his contemporaries made him a troublemaker. The Pharisees, scribes and other entrenched groups were not mistaken when they saw a man who had arrogated priestly – and even divine – privilege to himself.

By his supporters' own account, Jesus was crucified as a *lēstēs* – a robber or bandit.[29] This is the epithet religious conservatives applied to rebellious kinsmen – zealots whose activities imperilled everyone in the community. In this light, the part Jesus played in challenging the faith and beliefs of his contemporaries was, in the technical sense of the word, *satanic*. It bears repeating: 'the Hebrew term *satan* describes an adversarial role. It is not the name of a particular character.' The word could refer to 'any one of the angels sent by God for the specific purpose of blocking or obstructing human activity'.[30] What was Jesus' task if not to block or obstruct the activity of those who cleaved to inherited beliefs and practices? Nor should we forget that the satan numbers among the sons of God. From a traditionalist standpoint, the claims of the supposed messiah might represent a test for the pious to pass; if so, it would be only right to reject his presumption.

Impostors can appear at any place, at any time. Both Jesus' words and his person demanded thorough examination. Followers of the Christ, ancient and modern, would be the first to observe that the rude treatment he received made his virtues plain. This is why the cross, an instrument of slow and shameful death, has come to stand as the symbol of everlasting life.

Suspended Judgement

Like Job, Jesus was a scapegoat,[31] a pious man whose good deeds exasperated those less righteous than himself. In forgiving people who inflicted the greatest of wrongs on him, Christ proved his superhuman status. Even more than the healings he performed and the miracle of the Resurrection, his generosity to benighted persecutors demonstrated his divine nature. To hate one's fellow man is only human, after all.

The authors of the New Testament employed no small literary licence to make this point. When the Gospels were written, Judea had long been a seat of unrest. The First Jewish-Roman War, or 'Great Revolt', witnessed the destruction of the Temple in Jerusalem in 70 CE; uprisings continued for decades afterward – notably, in 115–17 and 132–5.[32] As far as the Romans were concerned, Jews were an unruly lot, and their internal squabbles held no interest. The legal historian Leonard W. Levy observes that the Gospels 'depoliticize all the titles ascribed to Jesus and present each in an exclusively spiritual sense.'[33] Anything redolent of temporal ambition would have alarmed the Romans; thus nearly all the lofty names that occur (such as 'Son of God' and 'King of the Jews') are found in speech attributed to others.[34] The evangelists sought to distance their nascent community of believers from other Jews, who did not think Jesus was the Anointed One.

The Gospels do not seek war on two fronts. Jesus instructs his followers to 'render . . . unto Caesar the things which are Caesar's, and unto God the things that are God's' (Matthew 22:21); unregenerate pagans were beyond reform, so they must be accommodated. Men and women who would 'walk in the light' (1 John 1:7) should avoid entanglements that keep them from leading pious lives. While conciliatory towards the Roman authorities, the gesture is provocative with respect to the Jewish establishment, which has made peace with unjust rulers.

Instead of presenting a political problem between the Jews and their foreign overlords, the evangelists attach all responsibility to the Sanhedrin, the Jewish legal assembly that condemns Jesus for refusing to admit he is not the Son of God. Reluctantly, the Roman governor Pontius Pilate goes along with the court's decision. However, it is impossible for such an event ever to have occurred. For one, historical record shows that 'the council had never before tried or convicted anyone for blasphemy.'[35] More importantly, the Sanhedrin would have had the authority to try Jesus only if the charges against him did not concern the Romans; in that case, capital punishment would have been carried out as per Jewish law, by stoning. Because Jesus was crucified, he must have been tried and sentenced by a Gentile court. Moreover, the real Pilate was not, as depicted, 'wise but spineless'. He was a 'cruel despot who slaughtered unarmed civilians, Jewish and Samaritan,'[36] and he would have had no qualms about doing away with another rabble-rouser.

Except when depicting the final execution of sentence, the Gospels basically omit mention of the foreign occupiers. The dramaturgy of the penultimate act is Jewish through and through. The Last Supper occurs at Passover, the commemoration of deliverance from Egypt. When Jesus offers his own life to followers present and future, he is renewing and 'updating' the holiday. The indignities that Jesus endures assume a meaning that extends beyond the fate of just one man. They recall the ancient history of Israel, written for the ages. Now as then, the Chosen People exhibit the traits of humankind in general: obstinacy and craven impulses.[37]

If the New Testament fulfils the Old Testament,[38] it does so by confirming the worst there is to say about human nature. Notoriously, Jesus is betrayed by Judas after Satan 'enters' his disciple (Luke 22:3, John 13:27). 'The Devil made me do it' – surely the lamest excuse of all time – would seem to have a biblical pedigree. But Judas does not take the easy way out. He repents and kills himself. Once again, the Greek original speaks of 'the satan' where translation produces 'Satan'. Everyone's nerves are being tried as the coming storm gathers. One person yields to a fit of perversity in a moment of weakness. No autonomous, malicious entity compels Judas; a flawed being, like all men and women, he assumes the role of 'the accuser' for a fateful instant, without really appreciating what he is doing.

Jesus already knows what will happen and that all his disciples will soon take flight. 'The true Light, which lighteth every man that cometh into the world' (John 1:9) shines on Jews and Gentiles, righteous, unrighteous or – as is the case for most human beings – some combination of not-very-good and not-entirely-bad. Loving people like that, and unconditionally, is the work of either a fool or a god among men.

TWO

Satan and Salvation

Jesus is tested and tried by Satan, yet the latter does nothing but defy him to perform actions he is unwilling to do. Not only does Satan commit no wrong; he sets the Messiah's glory into relief. It is mortal human beings who subject Jesus to the procedure that leads to his death. Mere men, they convict someone better than themselves and disavow responsibility for spilling blood by handing him over to others for execution. Jesus takes upon himself the imperfections of all who stand against him – those of his own kinsmen as well as the non-Jewish authorities. Thereby, he demonstrates his divine status, which Satan has verified.

This chapter explores the role of the Adversary in nascent Christianity. In passing from a minority cult to a universal religion, the new faith could not do otherwise than embrace struggle, setting its sights on something higher than the earth while offering guidance about how to live on it. When one heeds the voice of angels, existence represents a sanctifying ordeal. Believers prove their merit by enduring and overcoming hatred and hardship. In the Book of Revelation, which was originally written to consolidate Jewish ranks, Satan appears in the parted skies; the way through, and out of, this world leads through a portal only the newly chosen may enter.

The Darkness of the Light

Scholars disagree about the date to assign the Book of Revelation, and little is known about the man who wrote it.[1] John of Patmos, the author, was not the same person as the evangelist John of Zebedee, even though the popular mind has often confused them. The Book of Revelation may have been composed as early as 70 CE, but it was more likely begun two decades later. Either way, John witnessed events that invited reckoning on a global scale. War with the Romans and the destruction of the Temple in Jerusalem struck at the very heart of Judaism. Living 'among the nations' more than ever, the Jews faced the prospect of their age-old tradition going missing. Now that the earthly temple stood no more, religion had to be kindled within and shine forth in actions reflecting the glorious throne in heaven.

John of Patmos would not have seen himself as a Christian. He was convinced of the coming of the Messiah, long foretold and eagerly awaited. His words are addressed to his brethren, whom he sets apart from those who 'say they are Jews, and are not' (Revelation 2:9). John calls on his people to band together in the name of ancient truth.

The Greek word from which 'apocalypse' derives, *apokaluptein,* means 'to uncover'. 'Revelation', which comes from Latin, has the same sense: 'unveiling'. Apocalyptic discourse does not follow the standard rules of communication, but it does exhibit some generic features.[2] For one, the time and place of the visionary state fall outside the realm of everyday life. Second, revelation is hyperbolic. The images in which it trades shock and unsettle the profane. From the inception, the Book of Revelation employs language that guards the message it transmits. Only insiders can glimpse the meaning of darkly luminous speech. Hark the herald:

> I was in the Spirit on the Lord's day, and heard behind me a great voice, as of a trumpet, saying, 'I am Alpha and Omega, the first and the last . . . What thou seest, write in a book.'

John turns and beholds an otherworldly being:

> His head and his hairs were white like wool, as white as snow; and his eyes were as a flame of fire; and his feet like unto fine brass, as if they burned in a furnace; and his voice as the sound of many waters. And . . . out of his mouth went a sharp two-edged sword: and his countenance was as the sun shineth in his strength. And when I saw him, I fell at his feet as dead. And he laid his right hand upon me, saying unto me, 'Fear not' (1:10–17).

Rising from his own death, John finds himself on a higher plane of reality. What he has witnessed and now passes on to others revives a call pronounced during tribulations that his ancestors, and those of his intended audience, once faced.[3]

The prophet describes sights and sounds in a cosmic whirl. It is all but impossible to keep track of, much less process, the rapid succession of scenes. But inasmuch as the images unite in 'one like unto the Son of man' (1:13), order comes into focus: a solar system with stars circling the sun (1:16). Apocalypse suspends the regular flow of events and summons forth deep time. It not only records the author's experience of lapsing into unconsciousness and reawakening with keener awareness; it presents personal eclipse as a sign of self-renewal on a universal scale. Microcosm and macrocosm fuse for a moment portending eternity.

The combination of vividness and vagueness leaves it to listeners/readers to correlate the visions with what they know; to the extent that they make the necessary connections, they come to occupy the same plane as the seer. Bit by bit, the narrative discloses a tableau containing past, present and future in symbolic form. By turns, John expresses puzzlement and insight; patches of obscurity and flashes of light correspond to the states of mind one experiences trying to understand his words. Early on, a formula is repeated again and again: 'He that hath an ear, let him hear what the Spirit saith' (2:17, 2:11, 2:29, 3:13, 3:16, 3:22). Revelation means undergoing the rigours of a sacred agony. As the account proceeds, the truly faithful – those who observe 'the patience of the saints' (15:12; cf. 13:10) – undergo initiation into divine dispensation.

The first half of the Book of Revelation makes no mention of Satan. The heavenly messenger appears to John and instructs him to record what he witnesses for the 'seven churches which are in Asia' (1:11); instructions for each of them follow. Next, the prophet beholds the opening of celestial gates. Twenty-four elders are seated around the Throne of God, as well as 'four beasts full of eyes before and behind' (4:6). None has been 'found worthy' (5:4) to read the 'book . . . sealed with seven seals' in 'the right hand of him . . . on the throne' (5:1). John weeps bitterly but then is overjoyed to see, 'in the midst of the throne and of the four beasts, and in the midst of the elders . . . a Lamb as it had been slain, having seven horns and seven eyes' (5:6); this being, a visionary form of the Redeemer, has the power to accomplish what 'no man in heaven, nor in earth, neither under the earth' (5:3) can do. Terrifying events attend each unsealing (most famously, the

Four Horsemen of the Apocalypse); with the last, 'seven angels … before God' receive 'seven trumpets' (8:2). The angels sound their instruments and further woes beset the earth. An awful silence fills the air. Finally, the seventh trumpet blows:

> And there were great voices in heaven, saying, 'The kingdoms of this world are become the kingdoms of our Lord, and of his Christ; and he shall reign for ever and ever.' And the four and twenty elders, which sat before God on their seats, fell upon their faces, and worshipped God, saying, 'We give thee thanks, O Lord God Almighty, which art, and wast, and art to come; because thou hast taken to thee thy great power, and hast reigned. And the nations were angry, and thy wrath is come, and the time of the dead, that they should be judged, and that thou shouldest give reward unto thy servants the prophets, and to the saints, and them that fear thy name, small and great; and shouldest destroy them which destroy the earth.' And the temple of God was opened in heaven, and there was seen in his temple the ark of his testament: and there were lightnings, and voices, and thunderings, and an earthquake, and great hail (11:15–19).

The strange details and shifting perspectives drive away the vulgar and draw in those who know, if nothing else, that these words are a clarion call. Figures, numbers and phrases just keep adding up, and it is impossible to compute them.

In other words, the Book of Revelation is engineered to winnow out parties unfit to hear its message. A vast and complicated dramaturgy frames Satan's entrance, which occurs at a culminating point midway through the book. When the

Adversary takes the stage, he does so at high noon, so to speak. A constellation lights up the sky:

> There appeared a great wonder in heaven; a woman clothed with the sun, and the moon under her feet, and upon her head a crown of twelve stars: And she being with child cried, travailing in birth ... And there appeared another wonder in heaven; and behold a great red dragon ... [And] the dragon stood before the woman which was ready to be delivered, for to devour her child as soon as it was born (12:1–4).

The crown with twelve stars symbolizes the tribes of Israel. Its bearer, a 'woman clothed with the sun', points both to Eve, the mother of humankind, and to Mary, the mother of Israel's Anointed. The red dragon – Satan – stands for the obstacles confronting keepers of the Covenant then, now and in times to come. The Woman and the Dragon represent cosmic principles in tension.

At long last, the riddling Book of Revelation has proposed a formula for understanding the universe: a ceaselessly renewed battle between opposing forces united in terrible mystery.[4] This model explains the secret pulse of the world.

> And there was war in heaven: Michael and his angels fought against the dragon; and the dragon fought and his angels, and prevailed not; neither was their place found any more in heaven. And the great dragon was cast out, that old serpent, called the Devil, and Satan, which deceiveth the whole world: he was cast out into the earth, and his angels were cast out with him (12:7–9).

The 'war in heaven' does not represent a historical phenomenon, an event given within the time-bound dimensions of human intelligence. It represents a scheme for viewing the ups and downs of mortal existence as iterations of a single timeless struggle that will return again and again until all history ends.

Satan is still the 'intimate enemy' he has always been, testing the Chosen People.[5] Even if he 'deceiveth the whole world', those who have heard the prophet's speech should not be fooled. The combat between superhuman entities that John invokes is not so much physical as metaphysical. The hallucinatory visions capture inner realities: the toil and trouble assailing the hearts and minds of the elect, ever at odds with themselves and with others.

As Henry Ansgar Kelly observes, Satan 'was originally author-ized to be the official Accuser of Humankind'; in the Book of Revelation 'he still holds this position'.[6] As elsewhere in the Bible, the Adversary fits into a broader scheme of reasoning and design. His plunge from the skies points to the 'fallen', or imperfect, state of temporal affairs in general. In this light, it is only logical to equate him with 'that old serpent' from Genesis. Creation remains inferior to its Creator. Satan/the satan stands for ongoing strife, contention and trial, not malice.

John declares that these conditions, which define the world as human beings know it, will one day be over – and probably sooner rather than later. Then, and only then, will Satan/the satan be 'totally discredited and removed'. For the moment, '[his] ouster from heaven has not yet happened',[7] just as the destiny of the Jews must yet be realized.

If time (at any rate, time as mortals understand it) existed for God and His angels, they would have a perishable substance and not be divine at all. The inaugural formula repeated at the end of the Book of Revelation – 'I am Alpha and Omega' (22:13) – underscores that this is not the case. The prophet has no choice but to use human language to express what surpasses human understanding until history aligns with eternity. In the meantime, divine and diabolical scourges are not always easy to tell apart. 'As many as I love, I rebuke and chasten: be zealous therefore, and repent' (3:19).

Beastly Omens

Although the Book of Revelation did not remain a Jewish work in Jewish hands, it was meant for the Jews and no one else.[8] References to Babylon and Rome inscribe the visions in the struggles of a people destined to serve the Lord like no other nation. John tells how he has seen the pious assembly of 'one hundred and forty and four thousand' – 12,000 people from each of the twelve tribes of Israel – intoning 'the song of Moses the servant of God, and the song of the Lamb, saying "Great and marvelous are thy works, Lord God Almighty"' (15:3). There is no room for outsiders here. While events are universal in scope, only the actions of the few really matter. The Adversary looms large because, now as before, he works to confound those who are chosen but undeserving. Indictments of the 'synagogue of Satan' (2:9, 3:9) take aim at groups that claim to have inherited the mantle of the elect without abiding by the laws of the Hebrew Bible.[9]

John seeks to rally the righteous and steel their resolve as cataclysm approaches. At the outset, he declares that 'the time is at hand' (1:3). Imagery of cosmic ruin abounds: 'the great winepress of the wrath of God' will make blood pour (14:19–20). But if Final Judgement is imminent and urgent in absolute terms, the picture may yet prove otherwise on a human scale. All that John says draws its meaning from a source that escapes everyday reason.

In principle, 'things which must shortly come to pass' (1:1) can be deferred indefinitely; centuries and millennia amount to less than seconds for the Deity. All the same, mortals should not count on a reprieve. 'He that is unjust, let him be unjust still: and he which is filthy, let him be filthy still: and he that is righteous, let him be righteous still: and he that is holy, let him be holy still' (22:11). The unjust, the filthy, the righteous and the holy all have been warned. 'Behold, I come quickly . . . to give every man according as his work shall be' (22:12). All bets are off: one's every deed, each day of remaining life, counts.

The quasi-cinematic visions come so fast that they defy immediate comprehension. However, they reward calm and measured contemplation. Without presuming to have cracked the code of the Book of Revelation, we can connect the fantastical images within the text and find external points of reference, too. As in the Hebrew Bible and Gospels, Satan does not intervene in earthly affairs so much as he attends them in the capacity of a presiding official. His presence is negative. It stands beneath the dignity of a 'son of God' to dirty his hands. Satan, a spiritual entity, should not be equated with the terrible beasts John now describes.

When the prophet tells how he 'saw a beast rise up out of the sea', he is speaking in more concrete terms than one might think.

And the beast . . . was like unto a leopard, and his feet were as the feet of a bear, and his mouth as the mouth of a lion: and the dragon gave him his power, and his seat, and great authority. And I saw one of his heads as it were wounded to death; and his deadly wound was healed: and all the world wondered after the beast. And they worshipped the dragon which gave power unto the beast: and they worshipped the beast, saying, 'Who is like unto the beast? Who is able to make war with him?' . . . [And] power was given him over all kindreds, and tongues, and nations (13:1–7).

The word for 'beast' here, *thērion* in Greek, means 'vicious beast' or 'wild animal'. A milder term, *zōa* (simply 'animals', or 'living creatures'), is used for the 'four beasts' that stand 'round about the throne' and 'give glory and honour and thanks to him . . . who liveth for ever and ever' (4:9). This intrusive beast combines features of different animals, reflecting the turbulent element from which it emerges. An embodiment of chaos, it symbolizes imposturous rule in contrast to the 'Lamb . . . having seven horns and seven eyes', whose appearance is uncanny but not horrifying. In heaven, 'a sea of glass like unto crystal' (4:6) signifies order and calm.

The wild beast holds power from the dragon, but it does not act at the latter's behest. The beings correspond to two planes of reality with different quotients of metaphysical substance. The monster from the sea represents a second-order phenomenon subordinate to 'that old serpent, called the Devil, and Satan'. The spirit of contention is fine in service to the Lord, but unwelcome when it circulates freely. When John declares that dominion over 'all kindreds, and tongues, and nations' falls to the beast, he is indicting the world for lapsing into fractiousness and misrule. The fact that it occupies a seat and holds great authority means that people follow a law that is capricious and cruel – in other words, no law at all (again, in contrast to the scene before the heavenly throne). Like the hydra of Graeco-Roman mythology, the wild beast incarnates and thrives on discord.

Worship of this violent force is anti-religion, not an actual cult. What it yields is just as impermanent as the surf crashing on the shore. The next part of the vision underscores the vanity of practices dedicated to nothing, that is, the nullity of persons and institutions oblivious of the one true God:

And I beheld another beast coming up out of the earth; and he had two horns like a lamb, and he spake as a dragon. And he exerciseth all the power of the first beast before him, and causeth the earth and them which dwell therein to worship the first beast . . . [And he] deceiveth them that dwell on the earth . . . saying to them . . . that they should make an image to the beast, which had the wound by a sword, and did live. And he had power to give life unto the image of the beast, that the image of the beast should both speak, and cause that

Unknown artist, *The Beast Enthroned* (welcomes admirers and dismisses those faithful to God), *c.* 1255–60, tempera colours, gold leaf, coloured washes, pen and ink on parchment (MS. LUDWIG III 1, fol. 24v).

as many as would not worship the image of the beast should
be killed (13:11–15).

The second *thērion* does not represent an entity different from the
first so much as it articulates the same problem with a change of
emphasis. The two wild beasts are same thing: nothing real in
light of the heavens, just the tumult of ungoverned matter. This
monster makes 'the earth and them which dwell within to worship
the first beast'. The phrasing indicates that it draws its power from
deception: it has 'two horns like a lamb' yet '[speaks] as a dragon'.
The second beast is identical in essence to the first, just bigger
and badder, for it can 'give life' to falsehood and 'cause . . . as many
as [do] not worship the image of the beast . . . [to] be killed'. John
is issuing a warning on two registers: against idolatry, as per
ancient Jewish law, and against an antichrist – that is, a leader
superficially resembling the Lamb of God (this beast has 'two
horns') but spouting an unholy message.

Throughout the Book of Revelation, Satan remains the satan
– a shadowy figure in service to God's plans, not an independent,
self-willed actor. Even as the great red dragon, he does not perform
an evil role to his own ends. In the parlance of modern physics,
potential energy is not the same as kinetic energy. The beast from
the sea represents what happens in the absence of just rule. The
sea stands for disorder, and so does all that emerges from it. If
and when 'Satan . . . deceiveth the whole world', those who should
know better have not fulfilled their God-given duties and have
allowed themselves to be tricked. All ills come about through
human impiety and vice.

Only because people believe that no one 'is like unto the
beast' can the monster sit firm in its 'seat'. The extent to which

it exercises dominion depends on the credit that mortals grant it. John is writing in a kind of shorthand notation in order to describe things that reach beyond human ken.

John declares that the beast 'causeth all, both small and great, rich and poor, free and bond, to receive a mark' (13:16); he 'that hath understanding' should 'count the number of the beast' (13:18). Efforts to decrypt this enigmatic phrase are legion. The Roman emperor Nero, notorious for crimes against all and sundry but particularly against the followers of Jesus, counts as a prime candidate.[10] Yet trying to find a straightforward answer risks missing the broader truth. The number of the beast is finite, 'the number of a man' (13:18). What stands at issue is deifying a mortal – in principle, taking any human being for a god.

Prophetic discourse features *types*: symbols that are urgent now because they point to eternal forces. Their essence is old and, as a kind of ancestral memory, familiar. A stereoscopic perspective resolves contradiction and lends clarity to John's visions, including that of 'a woman . . . upon a scarlet coloured beast'.

> And the woman was arrayed in purple and scarlet colour, and decked with gold and precious stones and pearls, having a golden cup in her hand full of abominations and filthiness of her fornication: And upon her forehead was a name written, 'Mystery, Babylon the Great, the Mother of Harlots and Abominations of the Earth' (17:2–5).

The rider incarnates the seductive ills to which earlier generations of the Jewish people succumbed in foreign captivity. 'The Mother of Harlots and Abominations' represents the antithesis of the 'woman clothed with the sun', malign forces that once caused many of the chosen to betray the Covenant – and now threaten to do so again. The spectacle of 'Babylon the Great' involves what 'was, and is not, and yet is' (17:8), dangers of the past still at work in the present.

The heavenly messenger explains the mystifying sight:

Wherefore didst thou marvel? I will tell thee the mystery of the woman, and of the beast that carrieth her, which hath the seven heads and ten horns ... The seven heads are seven mountains, on which the woman sitteth ... And the ten horns which thou sawest are ten kings, which have received no kingdom as yct; but receive power as kings one hour with the beast. These have one mind, and shall give their power and strength unto the beast (17:7–13).

These words are more opaque to readers today than they would have been to John's contemporaries. The seven heads of the beast that the woman is riding represent the seven mountains for which Rome is famed; scarlet and, more still, purple stress the connection to the house of Caesar, whether occupied by Nero or another emperor.[11] The ten horns signifying ten kings point to separate stages of trial under different rulers, who all incarnate a single principle ('one mind') providing power and strength to the beast, so long as Creation stands. But Creation is *created*; a higher mind commanding greater power and strength will sweep it away.

Those with whom revelation has been shared must respond. The messenger from the skies affirms both ancient belief – the truth already disclosed in the Hebrew Bible – and a new prophecy.

Rome is currently the enemy, as Babylon was in its day. Whether by seduction or violence, it menaces the unity of God's elect. This front is relatively clear. At the same time, however, a rift has opened between those who abide by the Covenant and those who do not. Here, the lines are not so distinct: 'intimate enemies' abound.

The Book of Revelation only seems to promote Satan to the status of Counter-God, a cosmic force rivalling the Lord Himself. The Adversary's coming poses a challenge. All who pay heed and ready themselves for battle may be assured of belonging to the one true synagogue that has existed for ages. Despite – indeed, because of – the 'tribulation' and 'poverty' they face, they are 'rich' (2:9). Their brethren who fail to open their eyes to see the world in a new and ancient light are doomed. The faithful must prove themselves *now*, just as their ancestors did *then*. 'New Jerusalem' (21:2) awaits.

Enemies of All

The prophet's words did not become Jewish coin. Their further history belongs to the 'Jesus movement' within Judaism that, by opening the door to outsiders, came to constitute Christianity.[12] Its genius – that is, the spirit that ultimately made one sect among others a religion open to all – shone forth when harsh realities changed into the promise of salvation. The shift from woe to weal assumed political dimensions in the fourth century CE. Constantine I, who reigned from 306 to 337 CE, recognized that the Christian God and the ardour He inspired could serve his own military purposes.[13] Within a few decades, the formerly persecuted faith was the official religion of the Roman Empire.[14]

Matthias Gerung, 'John the Evangelist's Vision of God on his Throne, Surrounded by the Twenty-four Elders and the Four Beasts', one of 48 woodcuts from the series *Apocalypse and Satirical Allegories on the Church*, 1546.

This reversal of fortune was fraught, and it did not occur all at once. Among Jews, the message Jesus brought failed to inspire general enthusiasm. Inasmuch as those who followed the supposed messiah were enjoined to observe even the 'least commandments' – that is, to follow Jewish law and 'exceed the righteousness of the scribes and Pharisees' (Matthew 5:19–20) – Christianity competed with its parent religion. Willingness to indulge apostates loyal to a deified leader who had upset tradition proved limited, especially since it stood to worsen already poor political conditions.

But what could a pagan object? Because Christianity triumphed and hagiography risks passing for history, an excursus is warranted at this juncture. Whether they were 'good' or not, moral reasons existed to oppose the new faith. Even if Romans had no difficulty killing Jews and destroying the Jerusalem Temple, Judaism itself – a religion of demonstrable antiquity observed by a foreign people on their ancestral soil – did not represent a problem. Only when the natives grew restless was repression warranted. In contrast, the proselytizing splinter group of growing size – the 'Jesus movement' – posed difficulties.

Minucius Felix (who probably died around 250 CE) was one of Christianity's earliest apologists. His dialogue *Octavius* stages a debate between a believer and a pagan. Although the exchange is a work of fiction, the claims and arguments reflect divergent cultures and mindsets that were quite real. Before their religion was protected, Christians adopted an air of secrecy. While this measure afforded security, it also compounded danger. Because practitioners of the strange new sect veiled their activities, outsiders had no information that would contradict unflattering hearsay – or outright lies. Those of a censorious disposition interpreted the little they had seen or heard in terms of ready stereotypes of transgression and lawlessness.

Caecilius, the defender of the Roman gods, has heard shocking reports, which he shares with his interlocutor. Christians, it is said, 'consecrate and worship the head of an ass, the meanest of all beasts', and they 'reverence the private parts' of the priest officiating at their rites.[15] Something more unspeakable still occurs when members are inducted into the community of worship:

> An infant, cased in dough . . . is placed beside the person to be initiated. The novice is thereupon induced to inflict . . . blows upon the dough . . . and the infant is killed . . . The blood . . . they lap up greedily; the limbs they tear to pieces eagerly; and over the victim they make league and covenant, and by complicity in guilt pledge themselves to mutual silence.

As if murdering children and eating them were not enough, it seems that Christians practise further sacrilege:

> On the day appointed they gather at a banquet with all their children, sisters, and mothers, people of either sex and every age. There, after full feasting, when the blood is heated and drink has inflamed the passions . . . [the] light is extinguished, and in the shameless dark lustful embraces are indiscriminately exchanged.

If even some of the stories are accurate, there is no defending the terrible cult. What's more, its ranks include many unlettered people of lowly birth; how could anyone like that attain insight into the divine world?

Octavius the Christian counters the allegations with subtlety befitting a Devil's advocate – one who defends an apparently indefensible position. Lending his voice to the author's own views, he demonstrates the folly of believing in many gods and, more to the point, of relying on popular opinion and prejudice. Plato held that a single intelligence guides the universe, as did Aristotle. Before and after them, philosophers have posited a divine principle, even if they contradict each other – and sometimes themselves – by giving it different names. Moreover, Christianity's appeal to the uneducated betokens a kind of elegant simplicity that dispenses with tales of the gods which no one believes, anyway. None of the wild rumours are true. He and his co-religionists are the victims of calumny.

Caecilius recognizes valid arguments when he hears them. A few of the finer points will require elucidation, he remarks, but they can be discussed later. The pagan more or less converts on the spot. *Octavius* shows the dialectical resolution of opposites, which are not as incompatible as they appear at first. Although it ultimately disqualifies them, the dialogue presents the reasons why non-Christians viewed the rapidly growing religion with apprehension and met it on hostile terms. This even-handed work accepts the charges before demonstrating that they are baseless. Faith follows from sound philosophy.

The far-fetched claims about Christians did make a certain amount of sense. Traditionally minded Romans were shocked by a religion that broke with practices of devotion that they, their families and their countrymen had observed since ages past. Two ready models for actions that violate the laws governing society are cannibalism and incest. It is logical that pagans sought to make breaches of order intelligible along the lines of their own culture and heritage; images derived from mythology – Oedipus' murder of his father and marriage to his mother, and Thyestes' feasting upon his own children – would explain why members of this evil religion guarded secrecy. While inaccurate, such parallels stemmed from a valid concern: departure from norms that had held communal life together since time immemorial invited reprisal from the gods. By rejecting the cult that others observed, Christians stood to cause trouble for everyone.

Indeed, the charges had a basis in the faith's teachings. Christians worship one God instead of many, yet Christ was born a man – and he died like one, too. At his final meeting with his disciples, Jesus speaks of his blood and flesh as an offering in the rite of Passover. In a Jewish framework, the symbolism is clear: he is providing spiritual sustenance to the faithful. But if one is unfamiliar with Jewish tradition and takes the words literally, they sound like an invitation to anthropophagy.

The reports of orgiastic coupling among Christian worshippers are also cogent. In hyperbolic form, the slander expresses the concern that this religion not only runs counter to life but actually destroys it. The sexual perversions alleged of Christians would undo familial bonds and, with them, the hierarchy and reproductive cycles ensuring the continuity of civilization. Christianity menaces past, present and future. Inasmuch as the faith spreads through proselytization, illicit beliefs and practices will erode the social fabric.

The historian Peter Brown identifies 'a certain symbolic truth' underlying 'the bizarre . . . slur' shared by the philosopher in *Octavius*.[16] Christians really did 'reverence the private parts' of the presiding priest. Because their religion embraced chastity, it had a fixation on sexuality, albeit in a negative way. Strict continence mortified the flesh to promote detachment from earthly existence.

> It was a matter of vital importance for the believer that a body capable of bearing the Spirit of God within the Christian assemblies, in times of peace, should be enabled, also, through Christ and His Spirit, to endure ... the torments of a martyr's fate. Only Christ and His Spirit dwelling deep within them could enable men and women to resist the invasion of their souls and bodies by the overwhelming pain of torture and by the chill fear of death.[17]

Renunciation promised metaphysical renewal: rising above earthly desire for the ecstasy of everlasting life. A psychoanalytic interpretation would consider such a bearing a form of displaced sexual experience.[18] In any event, Christian asceticism mystified pagan onlookers, who reacted with horror.

For pagans, sexuality represented a force to be reined in; when properly managed, it was invested with 'portentous overtones of ideal order'.[19] The wholesale rejection of erotic impulses heralded disaster inasmuch as it expressed hatred for life in society, and even for life itself.[20] Accordingly, opponents of the new religion could claim, with a certain degree of accuracy, that Christian worship involved the destruction of children. Since it is natural for human beings to live in communities that propagate generation after generation (a word that is etymologically linked to 'genitals'), the faith represented an attack on the world as it had always existed. The religion of Rome assigned roles to individuals based on social position or the function they exercised; public acts were by nature religious, and vice versa.[21] Reverence for ancestors was sacred, too.[22] Christian contempt for the standing order inflicted universal injury. To the uninitiated, the cult seemed nothing but a great mass of transgression.

Meanwhile, Christianity drew on its Jewish roots to grow hale and hearty under adverse conditions. 'When my father and my mother forsake me, then the Lord will take me up' (Psalm 27:10). The Hebrew Bible abounds in reversals of fortune so miraculous that only the hand of God could have performed them. Joseph passes from being a favourite son into slavery; then, when in Egypt, he rises to a position second only to Pharaoh. His merits, which transcend those of ordinary human beings, point to a privileged connection with the divine sphere. A greater aura surrounds Moses, who accomplishes even more: wonders that found the Jewish religion itself. Moses has grown up among a people not his own and is likewise a 'stranger in a strange land' (Exodus 2:22). He rallies the oppressed, delivers them from bondage and gives them laws; thereby, the Israelites emerge as a united, self-possessed community. Other holy books feature dramatic changes between outsider and insider status. The story of Job offers a further example, as does the Book of Esther, which recounts how imminent doom turns into victory over those who would destroy the Chosen People. Such extreme shifts signify the power of the Deity to transform a downtrodden state into spiritual ennoblement and material rewards.

If Judaism had entered a covenant with God, Christianity made a covenant with Satan, God's legal officer. The wonder in the New Testament trumps all the tales of old. Sentenced to perish ignominiously, Jesus could not occupy a lowlier or more disgraceful position before he defeats Death itself through the miracle of the Resurrection. No part of this world-shaking event could play out in terms even remotely comprehensible to humankind without Satan, who, for all his apparent greatness and power, is still the lower-case satan of the Hebrew Bible.

The Saviour and the Tempter occupy the same symbolic space, and their contention throws the glory of God the Father into relief. The trial to which Satan subjects Jesus in the wilderness confirms the role and resolve of this *other* 'son of God'. When accused of casting out evil spirits in alliance with 'the prince of the devils', Jesus counters, 'How can Satan cast out Satan?' (Mark 3:22–3). Even intimacy and friendship do not guarantee concord; thus Jesus tells Peter, 'Get thee behind me, Satan: thou art an offence unto me: for thou savourest not the things that be of God, but those that be of men' (Matthew 16:23).

Such passages, along with the cosmic drama told in the Book of Revelation, gave early Christians comfort and strength as they faced internal dissension and external threats. Hardship, reimagined as testing at the hands of Satan, the Lord's deputy, armed the faithful and pointed to the path for attaining 'the holy Jerusalem, descending out of heaven from God' (Revelation 21:10). In the end, suffering signified that 'God dealeth with you as sons; for what son is he whom the father chasteneth not?' (Hebrews 12:7).

The Never-ending End

The Book of Revelation is the last part of the New Testament to have been canonized, and its meaning remains hotly contested.[23] Today, roughly two millennia after it was written, references to imminent cataclysm look embarrassingly dated, and descriptions of divine wrath, which conflict with the themes and tone elsewhere in the New Testament, suggest an 'unchristian' spirit. Yet the work was never intended for the profane. Whatever the finer points of the message might actually be, many of the righteous in the synagogue of Satan – Christians, who inherited the prophecy after the synagogue of God had rejected it – delight in the prospect of the only world they might ever know going up in flames.

Witches giving wax dolls to the Devil, woodcut illustration
in *The History of Witches and Wizards* (1720).

THREE

The Adversary at Home and Abroad

Today, the words 'Satan' and 'Devil' conjure up an abyss where the iniquitous expiate their sins amid blistering fires and black clouds of smoke. This was not always the case. There is no scriptural support for most of what now comes to mind about the dark corners of the afterlife.

In the Book of Genesis the act of Creation introduces a split between the heavens and the earth. A hierarchy emerges: one realm above and another below. But the Hebrew Bible does not portray heaven as a place of reward. Nor does it mention a terrestrial (or subterranean) place of punishment.[1] Celestial vaults and infernal caverns are Christian additions to the architecture of the universe. That said, the New Testament makes no mention of them. 'In my Father's house are many mansions' (John 14:2) does not refer to the layout of physical space; the words signify the possibility of salvation for all members of the human family.

No overlord of souls damned to the pit appears anywhere in the Bible. The Book of Job portrays the satan 'going to and fro in the earth', and other references to him in the Tanakh are set in the realm inhabited by human beings. The New Testament also shows the satan roaming about without a fixed address; if anything, he seems more incorporeal than he does in the Old Testament. The Book of Revelation includes mention of 'the lake of fire' (19:20, 20:10–15, 21:8), but this occurs in visionary time, without specification of its whereabouts.

Supernatural domains first obtained definition during the early centuries of the Common Era, when Christian theologians drew on pagan sources to situate human lives in a cosmic framework with morally charged divisions. It was later still, in the Middle Ages, that Heaven and Hell received a determinate geography and Satan, now a proper name more than a title, became more settled in his residence. On a tour of this world and the next, this chapter examines opposing yet complementary conceptions of the Adversary: a leaden but mighty potentate down underground and a crafty but frequently inept officer of the law up on the earth above. The two types derive from clerical sources and popular culture, respectively.

Cleansing Flames

First, a brief discussion of pre-Christian ideas about death and immortality is in order.[2] As it turns out, the pagan world never quite died.

In Graeco-Roman antiquity the departed belonged among the living, even if their mode of existence had changed. In day-to-day terms, religious observance had its *focus* – a word derived from Latin ('hearth' and, by extension, 'family' or 'household') – in the home.[3] The authority of the *paterfamilias* came from those who had gone before him; through the reverence that he and those in his charge paid to forebears, he already numbered in their ranks. In the *Aeneid* the importance that Virgil attaches to the hero bringing his *penates* (household deities) from Troy to Italy underscores this cardinal virtue. Piety, in the ancient sense of the word, refers to honour shown to parents and kin. Fulfilling this sacred duty ensured order on a larger scale among other men, who likewise owed their strength and status to their ancestors.

At the other end of the religious spectrum, the gods of the pantheon – Olympians gathered around 'Father Zeus' (or Jupiter, as he was known in the Roman world) – transcended clans, cities and regions. Because polytheism welcomed an infinite number of divine beings so long as the overall hierarchy went unchallenged, no competition occurred between the gods of the home and those of the state. It was always possible to accommodate other deities, including new ones; all received their due in keeping with their respective areas of influence.

The dead inhabited a proximate yet alien sphere that was not pictured altogether systematically. Hades/Pluto exercised dominion over them insofar as they warranted attention – most often for infamous deeds. Other deities held sway over the passage between the mortal and immortal realms, such as Hermes/Mercury, the divine messenger and guide of souls. After their demise, most people could expect anonymity and quiet domesticity to continue.

If respected, the departed would help the living, at least by staying calm; the woes plaguing the descendants of Atreus showed what could happen when ancestors were unhappy. The dead might even impart knowledge to exceptional individuals. Because death defies time and approaches the eternal, it offers a standpoint from which the view is clearer than what appears to clouded, mortal eyes. Thus, in Book XI of the *Odyssey*, the hero journeys 'across the River of Ocean' to reach the 'halls of Hades', where he encounters the shade of the seer Tiresias, who shares what his further travels hold in store. In Book VI of Virgil's epic, Aeneas descends to the underworld and beholds the glories of Rome ages before the city's destiny is manifest.

In contrast to the much older civilization of Egypt, where the vast house of the dead belonged to an elaborate system administrated by kings and priests and overshadowed the realm of the living,[4] the Graeco-Roman underworld was open-ended: sometimes terrifying, sometimes mirthful, but usually uneventful. No single vision, and certainly no canonical depiction, prevailed. Some philosophers did not believe in an 'afterlife' at all – or in the gods, for that matter.[5] Prominent figures could face an unwelcome version of life in the public eye. Aristophanes' riotous comedy *The Frogs* (405 BCE) depicts a place where merits and shortcomings are subject to definitive review – to the glory of Aeschylus and the shame of Euripides. Much later, in the second century of the Common Era, Lucian of Samosata (*c.* 125– *c.* 180) lampooned rulers and philosophical rivals in 'dialogues of the dead' that unmasked earthly pretensions to similarly humorous effect.

Pagan antiquity also knew so-called mystery religions, which were practised alongside domestic and civic worship and promised personal salvation to initiates. The best-known example in Greece was the Rites of Eleusis, which lasted from the time before Homer until the fourth century CE and centred on the mother-daughter pair of Demeter and Persephone.[6] In imperial Rome Mithraism – a cult deriving from pre-Zoroastrian religion in Persia – flourished, especially among soldiers.[7]

It might seem that Christianity represented just one mystery cult among others.[8] In fact, the faith drew strength from combining the worlds 'here' and 'there' into a simultaneous whole, infusing the mortal sphere with warmer intimations of immortality.

The central difference between the Christian worldview and those of other religious systems is a one-time miracle. The death and rebirth of a god has precedents and analogues elsewhere: Dionysos in Greek religion, for instance, or Osiris in ancient Egypt.[9] But the messianic and monotheistic framework inherited from Judaism gave (and gives) the concept a different value in Christianity. The Resurrection does not signify renewal – say, the turn of the seasons – so much as it marks a break in history that shines a brighter light on past, present and future. This singular event, the irruption of eternity into the created world, opens a portal between realms through which the faithful may pass.

Like other religions, Christianity denies that the dead are really dead. More importantly, it affirms that death *in* life is necessary. One must perish in order to rise again, sanctified and pure. Through the Christ's rebirth, death loses its sting (1 Corinthians 15:55). Incorporated into miraculous dispensation, the mortal wound heals. 'He that . . . believeth on him that sent me, hath everlasting life, and shall not come into condemnation; but is passed from death unto life' (John 5:24). The Father's incarnation as the Son upends the flow of generations and discloses a vertical dimension. Those who follow the Christ may, at least in theory, rise above the tide of coming-into-being and passing-away that engulfs the unredeemed.

Hence the importance of conversion in Christianity, from antiquity to the present. 'Becoming' a pagan was an absurd proposition and certainly not a matter of belief. The cults and practices were all there, ready to be observed – or not. One might elect to worship one or several deities in particular or be initiated in the mysteries, but the rites and sites of devotion were given. By the same token, one either was or was not Jewish by parentage and upbringing. Then as now, few Gentiles sought admission to the religion, which, in turn, hardly sought to recruit outsiders.[10]

Practising Christianity involved an act of will: actively renouncing received codes and prescriptions in order to complete a journey of transformation spanning worlds. In light of such striving, pagan mythology came to be seen as a distorted version or a foreshadowing of biblical events. The Old Testament no longer stood as the chronicle of a people so much as it provided a map of spiritual pilgrimage. The axial time of Christian religious experience lends itself to representation in spatial terms: the disorder of earthly events lies somewhere between a dead end at the bottom and serene rest at the top. Each pole corresponds to a different aspect of movement: churning strife on the one hand and airy sport on the other.

In this framework, the divine kingdom announced in the Hebrew Bible refers not just to a model society on earth, but to a beatific state in the hereafter.[11] At the same time, the warnings and injunctions voiced by ancient prophets come to bear on the followers of Christ. The people elected by God had the chance to walk with the Lord, but their every other step went in the wrong direction. Those who now *choose* to steer a righteous path in keeping with divine guidance might hope for better. Glad tidings do not exempt the faithful from hardship. There is still a test to pass: 'Satan hath desired to have you, to sift you as wheat' (Luke 22:31).

Mindful of God's exacting standards, the Devil's resourcefulness and the general fallibility of men and women, the Church needed to provide its flock with guidance. To this end, it offered a fuller picture of the higher reality beyond the confusion of the world apparent to humankind. Although the term 'Purgatory' did not appear until the twelfth century, when it was granted official status, the idea developed much earlier.

Jacques Le Goff credits Clement of Alexandria (*c.* 150–*c.* 215) and his younger contemporary Origen (*c.* 184–*c.* 253) with laying the foundations of Purgatory. These theologians drew on two resources: the achievements of pagan philosophy and the Bible. The former included the Platonic view that the quotient of truth and being of created things increases in proportion to their distance from matter; thus the form of an animal possesses more ontological substance than any given specimen (individual horses represent imperfect realizations of the transcendent type Horse). As Le Goff observes, 'Clement and Origen deduce[d] from this the idea that . . . any chastisement by God contributes to man's salvation' inasmuch as it strips away the contaminants tying one to the physical world. From the Old Testament the theologians 'took the notion that fire is a divine instrument, and from the New Testament the idea of baptism by fire'.[12] 'The voice of the Lord divideth the flames' (Psalm 29:7) and apportions justice. John the Baptist administers 'water for repentance' and declares: 'One more powerful than I . . . shall baptize you with the Holy Ghost, and with fire' (Matthew 3:11).

But the 'true father of Purgatory' was Augustine (354–430). Affirming 'the efficacy of suffrages for the dead' and thereby promoting contact between past and present,[13] the Bishop of Hippo reinforced the edifice of the faith. Unsettled accounts mortgage life on earth to a glorious future. By paying off others' debts, the present generation does right by its forebears and sets an example for those who will come after them; saving the universal family represents a collective effort. As an intermediary realm between temporal and eternal addresses, where souls undergo preparation for their ultimate due, Purgatory replaced Judaism's blood ties and journey across the desert with an ethnically mixed community headed upward unto 'mount Sion . . . to the city of the living God . . . and to an innumerable company of angels' (Hebrews 12:22).

In Augustine's words, the native terrain of humankind is a 'region of dissimilarity'.[14] Mortals are ever faltering on their unreliable perception and finite intellect. Many, if not most, sensory impressions and intellectual conceits lead them astray. The task of Christian religion is to help people find their way from the primitive security of the ancestral hearth, where it is warm but dark, up through purifying flames. Out from Plato's cave, as it were – where at most a vague likeness of reality can be discerned – souls emerge into brighter and brighter light until they behold wonders beyond Creation.

Pilgrimage to Hell and Beyond

The *Commedia* of Dante Alighieri (*c.* 1265–1321) performs a synthesis of some thousand years of Christian culture and learning. Every page of the *Divine Comedy*,[15] as it has come to be known, explores connections between the temporal and the eternal worlds as viewed by an itinerant soul. While autobiographical, the poet's journey also means to exemplify the path of mortals in general. This allegorical dimension, combining personal trials and universal lessons, is what lends Dante's vision its vitality, substance and enduring significance.

In terms of structure, the work has three orbits. The first is Inferno, the core of vitiated material existence; the second is

Purgatory, the proving grounds for imperfect souls; and the third is Paradise, the apex of 'intelligent design'. Each sphere realizes a different aspect of a single divine idea. Tellingly, Satan occupies the centre of the earth. Dante cannot begin travel upwards to God without facing – and surmounting – the lynchpin of obstacles on which so many men and women have foundered. Everything hinges on the nadir of all hopes.

The arrangement of the Inferno follows the principle of mounting guilt: increasing estrangement from a model existence spent in devotion to one's fellow man and to God. Lust is not as bad as greed, anger is not as bad as violence and so on. The voyage downwards culminates in treachery because this crime holds the most far-reaching effects for other human beings, now and forever. In the process of travelling through symbolically charged space,

Apprehensive demons look on as Christ enters their domain: detail from Andrea di Bonaiuto, *Descent of Christ to Limbo*, 1365–8, fresco in the Spanish Chapel of the Santa Maria Novella church in Florence.

where all that appears has a deeper meaning, the pilgrim must search his soul. Each spectacle he witnesses is the outcome of actions that a higher power has measured and weighed. In a sense, Dante belongs among the damned, for everyone in Hell has committed a sin within the scope of human error.

This other world that Dante visits holds many surprises, which shine new light on the mortal realm and the architecture of the cosmos. Divine providence and justice surpass what human beings can ever hope to understand. Accordingly, great pagans have escaped the worst of fates. The most accomplished authors of antiquity, as well as the great Islamic philosophers of the Middle Ages, inhabit Limbo – as do unbaptized children. Conversely, the netherworld teems with Christians, especially Dante's wicked contemporaries. The souls of the exceptionally depraved are already here while their bodies walk above.[16] Hell not only lies in store for the unrighteous; it overlaps with the earth as it stands.

For the greater part of the *Divine Comedy*, the pagan poet Virgil serves as Dante's guide. The author of the *Aeneid* identifies himself when he first takes the stage:

> I was born, though late, *sub Julio*,
> And lived in Rome under the good Augustus –
> In the time of the false and lying gods.
> I was a poet, and I sang the righteous
> Son of Anchises who had come from Troy,
> When flames destroyed haughty Ilium.[17]

Dante's purpose in making the poet of imperial Rome show him the way through Inferno and most of Purgatory represents more than a literary homage; it is also a matter of theological and political calculation. Like his contemporaries, the author of the *Divine Comedy* was aware that the 'modern' world still needed to live up to the achievements of antiquity. On the one hand, its civilization had honoured 'false and lying gods'. On the other hand, the Roman state reached great heights; as reference to 'the good Augustus' emphasizes, non-Christians can be morally admirable, too. When the poet-pilgrim enlists Virgil and the tradition he epitomizes, he does so to buttress his view of the cosmos with ancient authority.

The Inferno reflects the Christian universe, minus God's saving grace. As Dante and Virgil make their way through the rings of hell, the air grows darker and colder. When they reach their destination, the temperature stands at absolute zero. Identified by his erstwhile title 'Lucifer', the Adversary possesses towering dimensions: 'I match better with a giant's breadth / Than giants match the measure of his arms.'[18] Beating enormous wings as if he were a 'windmill',[19] Satan separates the good grain from the bad, 'sift[ing]' souls 'as wheat'.

Everything about the Fallen Angel looks like a warning more terrible than the famous inscription at the gates of Hell ('Abandon All Hope, Ye Who Enter'):

I marveled when I saw that, on his head,
He had three faces: one – in front – blood red;
And then another two that, just above
The midpoint of each shoulder, joined the first . . .
Beneath each face of his, two wings spread out . . .

. . .

They had no feathers, but were fashioned like
A bat's . . .

So that three winds made their way out from him –
And all Cocytus froze before those winds.
He wept out of six eyes; and down three chins,
Tears gushed together with a bloody froth.[20]

The faces dripping bloodstained tears perversely mirror the Trinity. The sole colour, other than pitch black and sickly white, is red, signifying a wound that will never heal. Satan's three mouths crush, in perpetuity, sinners who incarnate the depths of faithlessness: Judas, Brutus and Cassius. The first betrayed Christ; the second two conspired against Caesar and murdered him. They dangle there miserable and mauled, different aspects of the botched effort to undo the true order God has foreseen for all humankind.

Satan would appear to have been reduced to the condition of living death, condemned to perform the same movement over and over like a machine. Nothing about his condition inspires envy. All the same, his abjection signals grandeur. In the language of later times, Satan embodies gravity and ensures the equilibrium of the overall system. Testing and trial are key to the Lord's purposes. As ever, it falls to the Adversary to do the actual work. If left to its own devices, humanity would run riot. No wonder Satan looks exhausted and depressed: he is bearing the weight of the world.

Scholastic philosophy illuminates the new configuration of Satan's age-old role. *Summa Theologica*, by Thomas Aquinas (1225–1274),[21] explains how evil is possible in a cosmos where all things incline towards the *summum bonum*, or 'highest good'. Imperfection inheres in matter, which dwells at a remove from God, the transcendental Identity who made it. The closer any

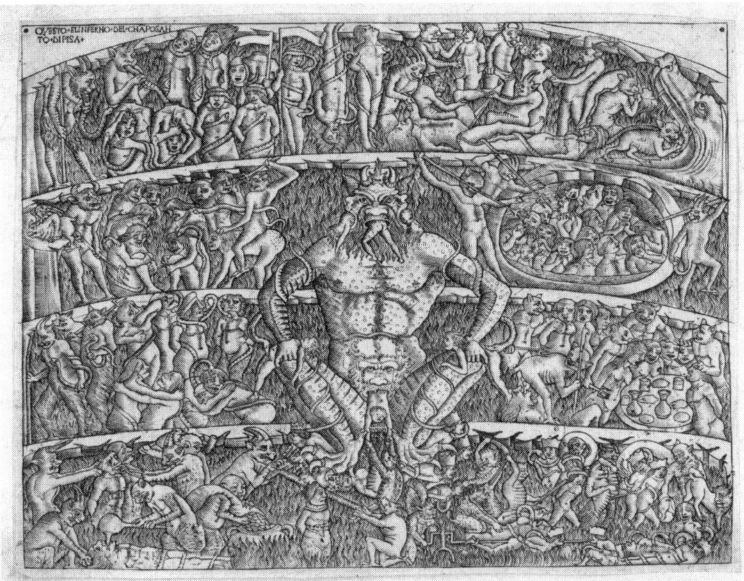

Anonymous, circle of Baccio Baldini, *The Inferno According to Dante*, 1481, engraving after fresco by Francesco Traini in Campo Santo, Pisa.

created thing stands to God, the *better* it is, in all senses of the word. Satan and his minions facilitate the natural human inclination towards wickedness, but they may be bested by a pious way of life.

Mortals must work to align themselves with divine will, directing their thoughts and actions upwards, lest they become entangled in snares that grow in proportion to distance from heaven. Paraphrasing Aquinas, a twentieth-century commentator has put the reasoning as follows:

God gives to men all requisite aid to repulse the assaults of demons, and to advance in grace and merit by resisting temptation. To the devil (who is the fallen Lucifer, now Satan) belong exclusively the plan and campaign of the demons' assaults upon mankind. In one way the devil is the cause of every human sin; he tempted Adam and thus contributed to the Fall which renders men prone to sin. But, in a strict sense, diabolical influence does not enter into every sin of man. Some sins come of the weakness of human nature and from inordinateness of appetites which the sinner freely allows to prevail.[22]

Men and women are fashioned in the Lord's image, and they have the inborn capacity to resemble their Maker and approach fullness of being. That said, they are only a *likeness* of the Deity. As creatures both physical and spiritual, they cannot bridge the gap and pass from similarity to identity. They can only lessen it by degrees. God represents one pole of human potential, and the Devil the other. 'The fallen Lucifer, now Satan' corresponds to humankind at its worst. Infernal beings inspire evil and prompt sinners to plummet deeper into base matter. Yet such 'assaults' give mortals the opportunity to prove their mettle, too.

If Satan represents 'the cause of every human sin' in an absolute sense, people remain accountable for allowing 'inordinateness of appetites . . . to prevail' in the sphere of contingency they inhabit. Aquinas distinguishes between 'theoretical' and 'applied' levels of operation.

Dante does the same. Thus *Inferno* shows clever demons besting wicked souls by turning their own sophistry against them. In Canto XXVII Guido da Montefeltro describes how he was whisked off to the pit despite having received papal absolution for the false counsel he gave. As 'one of the black Cherubim' observes, 'one can't absolve a man who's not repented, / and no one can repent and will at once; / the law of contradiction won't allow it.' The perfidious man is dumbstruck. 'Perhaps you did not think I was a logician!' his torturer sneers.[23]

Dante's cosmos consecrates the great cultural movements of the High Middle Ages. His map of supernatural order mirrors the push for systematization that occurred in theology around the same time. More still, it reflects – and reflects on – political events of the day. The battle between the Ghibellines, who supported the authority of the German emperor in Italy over that of the pope, and the Guelfs, who supported the papacy's temporal ambitions, forms an important subtext in the *Divine Comedy* – as does infighting within the latter group, to which the poet belonged. As a 'White Guelf', Dante held that papal over-involvement in worldly affairs disgraced a holy institution. When the 'Black Guelfs' took over in Florence, he found himself exiled from his native city.[24] While affirming the oneness of the Christian religion, the author of the *Divine Comedy* has no problem putting erstwhile allies and even popes in Hell.[25]

The contest between imperial and papal claims arose from the process of political centralization that took place throughout Europe as rulers with a greater sense of organization than local potentates consolidated power previously scattered among fiefdoms. Now, Satan invested a new role as the stand-in for government exceeding proper bounds. As Robert Muchembled observes, the Adversary 'evoked . . . the obverse of a well-regulated sovereignty'. Arrayed in the 'insignia' of legitimate rule, he represented 'corrupted majesty'.[26] Dante makes a point of calling Satan 'the Emperor of the kingdom dolorous'.[27]

In this context, the darkness of Hell depicted by Dante signifies its opposite, high above. 'Perfect disorder' prevails in the Inferno.

From a cosmic perspective, the flickers of suffocated light point to heavenly radiance. Likewise, the muffled sobs and discordant wails resemble an orchestra tuning up before a symphony. When the poet-pilgrim finally arrives in Paradise, he witnesses harmony beyond compare, a concert for all the senses.

The Wages of Sin, Fore and Aft

By and large, learned opinion granted little personality to Satan in the Middle Ages. Even if some devils had mastered dialectical argument, the Adversary and his retinue did not command discourse or persuasion in a full sense. Most activity was routine, like a degraded reflection of clerical bureaucracy.

Inferno features a host of creatures that carry out menial jobs in the underworld, a virtual horde of shuffling monks. Dante drew many of them from Graeco-Roman sources. They still have names, but the monstrous figures from classical mythology now lack personality and drive. Charon, the ferryman over the River Styx, sullenly recites imprecations as he performs his thankless task: 'Woe to you, corrupted souls! / Forget your hope of ever seeing Heaven.'[28] In turn, Geryon – the monster Heracles/Hercules confronted in his tenth labour – has been reduced to a kind of elevator between different circles; he no longer does anything of his own accord and says nothing at all.[29]

The picture is livelier where Dante's encyclopaedic work draws on folk belief and popular culture. The exploits of lesser devils provide a counterweight to quasi-robotic and largely mute functionaries with an ancient pedigree. Just before reaching the frozen wasteland where the erstwhile Lucifer is lodged, the poet encounters a bumbling gang. The name of the team, Malebranche, translates to 'evil claws', and the leader is Malacoda, 'evil tail'. One of them is called Alichino, a garbled version of *Arlecchino* (harlequin). Charged with supervising sinners stewing in pitch, the Malebranche provide a farcical interlude to offset the tragedy in the first part of the *Divine Comedy*. Whenever one of the damned tries to escape, a demon prods him in the rump and sends him back into the sulphurous broth. When not attending to their unlucky wards, the fiends fight among themselves. Clumsy members of the gang often wind up taking a bath in the filth. They seem like cats and dogs fighting, or drunken peasants.

Medieval culture made ample room for the grotesque, which represented a means of moral instruction more accessible to most people than the ratiocinations of the schoolmen.[30] While not as low as modern prejudice suggests, literacy was patchy under the best of circumstances, and even clerics might demonstrate inadequate mastery of the written word.[31] Hell and damnation are serious matters, but their import could be driven home through earthy humour, too.

The medieval Church was nothing if not expansive. In monastic tradition, the historian Jeffrey Burton Russell observes, 'the colorful ideas of the desert fathers predominated', and 'homilists dwelt upon the appalling for the explicit purpose of terrifying their auditors into good behavior'.[32] The legend of St Anthony represents a case in point. But in a less literate milieu, 'folklore … tended to make the Devil ridiculous.' Simple people clung to beliefs that recognized the Adversary's power. At the same time, they held that he could sometimes be eluded – or even beaten by ruse. The capricious nature deities inhabiting the European landscape before the arrival of Christianity lived on in transfigured guise, as playfully malicious spirits.[33] Such notions did not conflict with the Church's teachings: God made the world, so it is only right that humankind – which still harbours a trace of its divine origin – might occasionally avert evil by native wit.

The cathedrals erected throughout Europe during the Middle Ages made the supernatural dimension visible for clergy and laity, educated and uneducated, alike.[34] The collaboration of builders and artisans ensured that these temples included pious works from humble hands. Statues of the saints invited the faithful to enter another realm, where elaborately orchestrated services engaged all organs of perception. Rare fragrances of incense filled the air, hymns resounded in an echo of heavenly choirs and exquisite furnishings distilled the majesty of Creation into numinous objects. Pictorial representations of biblical history dispelled the mists of time blocking worshippers' views of archetypal scenes of trial and triumph.

Religious architecture suspended the rules of time and space governing everyday life and opened a glimpse of the hereafter. The Devil and his demons had a place in the pageantry, too. As a prelude to the mysteries inside hallowed halls, gargoyles on the outside offered taunts; in inclement weather their mouths poured down rain, like the sea-beasts of ancient lore taken to the skies. Looming on the altar wall, massive scenes of the Last Judgement included depictions of Satan devouring the wicked to illustrate the eternal stakes of flouting divine commandments.

The medieval conception of Satan was 'contradictory', then.[35] On the one hand, the Adversary promoted fear of God by incarnating terror. On the other hand, the Devil, especially as represented by his lesser agents, frequently proved laughable. The clichéd image of a world haunted by superstitious dread is half the picture at best.

The patience of a saint: Martin Schongauer, *St Anthony Tormented by Demons*, c. 1470–75, engraving.

Geoffrey Chaucer's *Canterbury Tales*,[36] written towards the end of the century that began with Dante's *Divine Comedy*, presents another account of pilgrimage. Diabolical influence taints everyone – including nominal servants of the Lord – yet religion emerges triumphant.

'The Friar's Tale' and its rejoinder, 'The Summoner's Tale', form a diptych of petty discord that reflects matters of real weight. Like all mortals, men who represent the Church are susceptible to sin. Friars had the job of circulating among the laity and ministering to its spiritual needs on a day-to-day basis. Summoners, in contrast, were more detached functionaries, responsible for serving notice when people ran afoul of authorities or were otherwise required to participate in legal proceedings. Neither class of official comes away looking particularly good in *Canterbury Tales*. Holiness and perversion walk side by side, animating each of the speakers in turn. First the one, then the other, indicts the group to which his rival belongs. Notwithstanding their squabble, the Church remains undiminished in dignity.

Chaucer's Friar takes the lead. The fact that he speaks to a summoner about *another* summoner (who is unnamed) gives his discourse the appearance of impartiality. Yet the Friar is attacking his listener for belonging to a class that exhibits shameful behaviour as a whole. His tale concerns a corrupt official who sets out to extort a woman, allegedly for committing adultery. The haughty man – who insists on the title 'bailly' instead of the 'filthe and shame' of being called only a 'somonour'[37] – abuses the power vested in him by clerical authorities for private gain. En route to his victim, the summoner encounters a devil masquerading as a yeoman. The 'feend' claims that he, too, is a bailiff, albeit in service to a manorial court. Even though the false yeoman openly declares that his 'dwelling is in helle',[38] the crooked summoner accepts that they are 'brothers'; he hopes to learn a trick or two from his confederate.

The man who means to hoodwink the guileless widow has met his match. When the exasperated woman utters an oath cursing him to damnation, the devil comes collecting. One is only as good – or as bad – as one's word. The summoner has been trading dishonestly, and now he must pay with interest. The demon is the agent of divine justice, a 'bailly' who understands the real duty of the profession.

The Summoner sees through his interlocutor's thinly veiled attack. If the Friar knows so much about devils, he counters, 'that is litel wonder', for 'freres and feendes been but lyte asonder' – that is, there's no real difference between them.[39] Before telling a tale of his own, the Summoner likens his fellow-traveller's kind to swarming 'bees' that seek personal profit everywhere on God's green earth. The 'hive' to which they bring their spoils lies under the 'tayl' of 'Sathanas'.[40] Friars do not make honey with the ill-gotten fruit of their labours.

'The Summoner's Tale' also concerns the abuse of power. The depraved Friar in this narrative makes a mockery of the vows to which he is supposed to adhere. Like his brethren, he has sworn to practice humility, embrace poverty and minister to Christians in need, yet he is proud, gluttonous and money-hungry. At the home of a poor man and woman whose child has recently died, he recognizes an opportunity. Hoping to impress simple people with his knowledge and holy airs, he claims to have known about their misfortune by dint of revelation, even before they told him.[41] He says that he has had his colleagues offer prayers for the departed and asks for a donation. The husband doesn't buy his story and pays him exactly what his hot air is worth: a fart. Foiled, the impostor buzzes off.

In 'The Friar's Tale', the Devil takes the stage as the trickster of popular tradition and circulates as any commoner would. 'The Summoner's Tale', on the other hand, presents a hulking monolith sulking in silence, Sathanas. The visions correspond to the respective offices of the narrators. The Friar has a summoner experience defeat when a lawyerly devil catches him on a technicality. In response, the Summoner – whose 'fyr-reed cherubynnes face' calls to mind an officer of Hell[42] – paints a picture in which the pestilential race of friars resides in Satan's hindquarters. For Chaucer, the underworld and its denizens both reflect and comment on the world of the living, offering a caricature of familiar misdeeds and the social types responsible for them.

It is no accident that both Dante and Chaucer crafted their works as narratives of pilgrimage. The proximity – if not consubstantiality – of Hell and Earth was not a matter of literary licence so much as an incontestable fact during the Middle Ages. People needed reminders to stick to the straight (but not always narrow) path of virtue. Especially in the space of literature and art, far more freedom of expression was granted than modern minds are likely to assume – provided, of course, that lessons about first and final things were taught in the process.

The Open Jaws of Hell

The Russian literary theorist Mikhail Bakhtin has offered a famous description of the dynamic contradiction at the heart of medieval culture:

One can say . . . [that] man lived as it were two lives: one – official, monolithically serious and gloomy, subordinated to a strict hierarchical order full of fear, dogmatism, veneration and piety, and another – carnival – vulgar, free, full of ambivalent laughter, blasphemies, profanations of everything sacred, lowerings and obscenities, familiar contact with everybody and everything . . . Without taking into account the interchange and mutual influence of these two systems of life and thought (official and carnival), it is impossible to understand correctly the peculiarities of medieval man's consciousness.[43]

During festivals, townspeople inhabited transfigured time and space. For a spell, internal differences and rivalries vanished. Carnival provided an experience analogous to that of the Saturnalia in pagan Rome, when social hierarchies were levelled; the New Year began with a re-enactment of the Golden Age prior to division and strife. The 'laughter' it brought offered a glimpse of eternity, a momentary realization of utopia.

The Church looked askance at spectacles, games and theatrical entertainments, rightly suspecting a heathen spirit. Yet official culture recognized the possibility of tempering the fun of make-believe with the solemnity of religious celebration. As E. K. Chambers notes in an authoritative study, *The Mediaevel Stage*, Christian worship displayed 'dramatic tendencies' from early on.[44] Because the laity was largely illiterate (and certainly did not know Latin, the sacred tongue of Western Christendom), Christmas and Easter were occasions for liturgical plays at houses of worship. Over time, performances extended to adjacent areas and expanded in scope, yielding a comprehensive 'cosmic' drama.[45]

Anonymous, 'Souls Released from Purgatory', *c.* 1440, folio from *The Hours of Catherine of Cleves* (MS M.917/945, fol. 107r).

Biblical events were staged with costumes, sets and special effects. With civic and professional pride, guilds took charge of portraying scenes of universal history, which unfolded before the eyes of their fellow Christians here and now. Smiths might perform one episode, while tailors took care of another, and so on. Cycles that could last for days drove home teachings that otherwise risked remaining disembodied and abstract. Even villainous roles – for example, the Roman soldiers mocking Christ on the cross – illustrated Scripture.

An integral component of medieval stagecraft was the hellmouth, which called the heavy price of sin to mind even amid merriment. As the name indicates, the hell-mouth represented the gaping jaws of an infernal beast into which the impenitent vanished. When costumed agents of the underworld dragged sinners off to eternal punishment, the crowd might laugh, but it shuddered, too. The foretaste of heavenly joys provided by general celebration had a forbidding pendant, reminding all and sundry of the stakes of (im)proper conduct. Such festivities corresponded to depictions of the Day of Judgement, which appeared in a variety of settings but especially in the panoramic frescoes that formed the backdrop for religious services. Here, below angelic choirs, gloating demons tortured the damned and pushed them into Satan's ravening maw.

The 'new birth of the drama in the very bosom of the Church's own ritual' during the Middle Ages may be viewed 'as one will, either as an . . . attempt to wrest the pomp of the devil to a spiritual service, or as an inevitable . . . recoil of a barred human instinct'.[46] In any event, the medieval Satan and his host were one with this world. As per conservative wisdom, there was a place for everyone. The Adversary performed the function that has always been his charge: to remind mortals that the Law applies to all created beings. Anyone who made bold to contend with infernal forces might win the occasional battle, but the war was lost. The silent hell-mouth spoke the final word on the wicked.

Doubt, Dissent and the Devil

In the Middle Ages, Satan sat in stony silence. His minions' chatter mirrored what was said by sinners, who undid themselves when infernal agents took them at their word. The giant hell-mouth in religious iconography and the sets of cycle plays did not talk. It vomited up demons and gulped errant souls down, illustrating the eternal stakes of theological doctrine for common people. Citadels of learning presented an Adversary who was just as mute: Satan was a principle more than a personality for scholastics like Thomas Aquinas; in Dante's *Divine Comedy*, he is covered in tears and gore in the bowels of the earth.

Movements at variance with Church doctrine had always existed,[1] but voices of dissent and protest gained traction and momentum during the Reformation. In its wake, the Anglican divine Robert Burton (1577–1640) could describe human consciousness as the site of perpetual conflict. His vast compendium of erudite agony, *Anatomy of Melancholy*, details how 'the devil reigns, and in a thousand several shapes'.[2] Burton's contemporary Shakespeare dramatized the condition. His prince of Denmark is positively terrorized by knowledge that 'the devil hath power / T'assume a pleasing shape',[3] and he stays his vengeful hand until action proves ruinous for him and everyone else. *Hamlet* sparkles with wit, yet the outcome is tragic.

In the sixteenth and seventeenth centuries Catholics and Protestants denounced their opponents for being in league with the Adversary. On the surface, such charges were straightforward: each group thought the other was acting at odds with God's will. Yet as we have seen, the biblical Satan (that is, the satan) does not work ill for the sake of evil; his doings, though unpleasant, conform to the Deity's higher plan. It is possible that both sides were right, if not quite in the way they would have claimed. Christians clamouring for the blood of their brethren fall into a diabolical snare: assurance that they are righteous when their own thoughts and deeds deserve punishment. Satan, the prosecutor of old, is free to do as he sees fit to enforce the law; the guilty will have eternity to howl that they are innocent.

Confession and Conjuration

Legend holds that Martin Luther (1483–1546) inaugurated the Reformation in 1517 by nailing his Ninety-five Theses to the door of the castle church in Wittenberg. A revolutionary priest pounding the tenets of a world-shaking vision onto sacred portals provides a commanding image for popular history, but this way of proposing debate was standard procedure. Warily noting that human efforts and institutions are flawed, Luther took issue with the sale of indulgences, submitting that accepting money in lieu of real contrition bespoke spiritual bankruptcy. He was not the first to see a problem here, and at this juncture he did not necessarily have schismatic intentions.

As Diarmaid MacCulloch observes, 'humanist scholars and serious-minded folk were horrified at the exceptionally vulgar emotional blackmail' of the Church's recent indulgence campaigns.[4] How can one account for the 'cataclysm' that Luther initiated, with or without a hammer?[5] Clerical corruption and rulers' greed, to say nothing of 'vague forces of modernity', have been offered as explanations. However, such factors do not add up to a necessary cause. 'Only . . . the explosive power of an idea' could produce an impact on this scale – to wit, 'a new statement' of Augustine's soteriology, or doctrine of salvation.[6] Like many of his contemporaries, Luther benefited from the recent edition of Augustine's works published in Basel by Johann Amerbach (1490–1506). What's more, he belonged to the order of Augustinians, named in honour of the Church Father. Both for reasons of personal temperament and on the basis of theological reflection, Luther was struck by what Augustine had said about inherent 'human worthlessness'.[7] The good Lord makes merciful provision for sinful mortals. In objective terms, no one merits leniency.

The charge that Luther detonated had been set long ago. On the one hand, the Church claimed power to save members who performed good works; on the other, patristic doctrine held that only divine grace could ever deliver beings inclined to wickedness. Significantly, he included a copy of the Theses in a letter of protest to Albrecht von Brandenburg, Archbishop and Elector of Mainz and Archbishop of Magdeburg, who had received papal dispensation for the sale of a plenary indulgence to settle debts in his benefices – which would also help finance the rebuilding of St Peter's Basilica in Rome. This missive, which Albrecht passed along to the pope, combined with the Theses' circulation, made a provincial dispute assume unanticipated scope as pamphlets and screeds multiplied. Not only did 'an independent public opinion' shape events; 'the printing presses which fuelled it could not be controlled by the existing hierarchies in Church and Commonwealth.'[8]

For some time yet, Luther endeavoured to demonstrate that his aims agreed with the standing order. His *Freedom of the Christian Man* (1520), for example, tempered the attack on institutional realities with deference to the person of Pope Leo X (who held the office from 1513 to 1521). 'Most blessed father, in all the controversies of the past three years I have ever been mindful of you,' the reformer began, endeavouring to maintain decorum and leave room for reconciliation. All the same, he was unable to contain the bile swelling within:

Did not Christ call his adversaries a generation of vipers, blind guides, and hypocrites? And did not Paul refer to his opponents as dogs ... and sons of the Devil? Who could have been more biting than the prophets? ... You may have three or four learned and excellent cardinals, but what are they among so many [others]? The Roman *curia* deserves not you but Satan himself. What under heaven is more pestilent, hateful and corrupt?[9]

Luther had a sharp mind and an even sharper tongue. As accurate as his references to Scripture were, and as much as he affirmed the personal probity of the pope, the image he presented – the Vatican infested with the brood of Hell – was hardly suited to winning over the leader of Western Christendom. Luther was acting in bad faith; that same year, he confided to a supporter that 'the pope is the adversary of Christ and the apostle of the Devil.'[10]

The Papist Devil: 'Ego sum Papa' (I am the Pope), anonymous engraving from a Reformation handbill against Pope Alexander VI, *c.* 1540, Paris.

Meanwhile, advocates of tradition denounced the league that the renegade monk – 'this Satan', as papal nuncio Girolamo Aleandro called Luther[11] – had formed with the forces of evil. In early 1521, soon after Luther publicly burned the papal bull *Exsurge Domine* ('Arise, O Lord') that threatened him with ejection from Christian society, Leo excommunicated the firebrand. In May secular authorities at the Diet of Worms banned Luther's writings and called for his arrest.

And that was just the beginning. The further course of events goes beyond what admits treatment here, but the foregoing is enough to identify the issues and battle lines of the coming years and decades. For Luther, living one's faith meant confronting the Adversary directly, wherever he showed himself. In 1521–2, Luther spent ten months hiding out in Wartburg Castle, penning jeremiads against the papacy and translating the New Testament while wracked by indignation and pain (from constipation, in particular). Here, the stain left by the inkwell he is supposed to have thrown at the Devil may still be seen on the study wall. The fight with Rome was just as polite.[12]

In brief, an 'accidental revolution' occurred when an obscure cleric in the German hinterlands asked whether salvation comes from obeying the dogma and ritual of the divinely instituted Church or from the mercy that God shows ardent believers.[13] The question, some thousand years old, had been asked before, and Luther was not the only one in his day to pose it. The latter's character and persistence, together with a specific constellation of social and political circumstances,[14] transformed an issue that might have remained an academic quarrel into a virtual apocalypse.

Above all, Luther wished to erect a fortress of piety and virtue to withstand the incursions of an institution that had grown estranged from its original purpose to pursue worldly aims. Indeed, he harboured reservations about the authenticity of the Book of Revelation until he recognized its usefulness for anti-papal polemics.[15] But other reformers embraced the prospect that the end was imminent; the hour for decisive action had struck. During the brief but fateful German Peasants' War, which erupted in the wake of the preceding years' comparatively decorous contests, Thomas Müntzer (c. 1489–1525) and likeminded radicals exhorted the meek to enter upon their inheritance by force.[16] A swift and terrible blade suppressed the plebeian crusaders, who were more or less armed with faith alone. At least 100,000 lives – if not souls – were lost. One hundred years later, at the centenary of the Reformation, the Thirty Years War (1618–48) erupted. As one authority puts it, 'never before . . . in [German] history had there been so universal a sense of irretrievable disaster, so widespread a consciousness of the horror of the period that lay behind.'[17] Still in the nineteenth century it was widely believed that most of the population had been killed.

Elsewhere in Europe, under the pressure of other personalities and political agendas, contention spread. Long ago, competing Jewish sects had tarred kinsmen who flouted the ways of the Lord with the brush of Satan.[18] Now, Catholics and Protestants alike could find plenty of evidence to confirm that the Adversary was afoot and contriving their doom through the actions of rival Christians. Confessionalism meant incompatible ways of trying to please God. Throughout the struggle, Satan was on everyone's lips, accusing *everyone else* of nursing evil in their hearts.

In France the Wars of Religion from 1562 to 1598 caused the death of millions.[19] The slaughter concluded with the Edict of Nantes, which granted practitioners of reformed religion legal rights while affirming France's essential Catholicism. Its signatory, Henry IV (1553–1610), had been baptized in the Catholic faith but raised a Protestant. Tolerance and/or political gamesmanship cost him his life. After surviving some dozen assassination attempts, 'Good King Henry' was killed by a fanatic who thought that the 'most Christian King of France and Navarre' was starting a war against the pope. 'The children of this age have Satan for a nursemaid,' lamented the poet Agrippa d'Aubigné (1552–1630).[20]

Reformation in England had begun in earnest when another Henry, Henry VIII (1491–1547), sought to have his marriage to Catherine of Aragon annulled for want of male issue.[21] Thomas Cranmer (1489–1556), the Archbishop of Canterbury, marshalled his theological and institutional muscle to aid the king in this personal, political and economic enterprise. The coronation of Henry's nine-year-old son, Edward VI – a Protestant born and bred – permitted Cranmer to work wonders against 'Satan' and 'his subtle servants': 'monks, friars, nuns, and other pope-holy hypocrites.'[22] In turn, Edward's successor Mary I (1516–1558) went after Protestants (hence the epithet 'Bloody'). Cranmer stood trial for treason and was condemned to death. John Foxe's enormous *Actes and Monuments* (1563) records his martyrdom, as well as that of countless others. The number of the sanctified – or infamous – dead would only grow.

What Cranmer wrote in 'A Confutation of Unwritten Verities' (*c.* 1556) might have been said by combatants across Europe on either side of the epoch's spiritual and material battles. 'As the true church of Christ can never be long without persecution, in like manner can the false church of Satan . . . never cease from persecuting.'[23] Like the 'two-edged sword' from the angel's mouth in the Book of Revelation (1:16), the charge cut both ways.

The Soul for Sale

The Reformation was heaven-sent for Satan. Allegiances shifted for reasons of conviction or opportunity, expectations were not necessarily realistic and channels of communication could always prove less than ideal.[24] Luther surprised many contemporaries by siding with the nobility when the peasantry took up arms. On the whole, he did not show much interest in affairs of state, but if the Lutheran church never spread far beyond German-speaking territories, the effects were felt for centuries to come. In contrast to Luther, the French reformer John Calvin (1509–1564) had civic concerns – even though Geneva, the city that enacted his *Ecclesiastical Ordinances* (1541), did not always welcome him.[25] In England Henry viii broke with Rome, dissolved the monasteries and seized their property, but he despised Luther.[26] Discord thrived as theological subtleties, political calculations and chance events made and unmade human fortune. No uniform scheme explains events that appear inevitable in retrospect. Chaos is a boon for devils.

Johannes Gutenberg's invention of movable type in the mid-fifteenth century, which marks a historical turning point in its own right, played a key role in developments by allowing 'satanic' rhetoric and colourful, diabolical libels to flourish. Luther and his associates would not have been in the position to broadcast their ideas without the printing press, and they might not have arrived at some of them in the first place if, like their medieval forebears, they had been able to consult writings only in manu-script. The early modern media revolution accelerated social change.[27] Vernacular literature, which grew thanks to the trans-lation of the Bible and educational initiatives on the part of both

Danger all around: Albrecht Dürer, *Knight, Death and the Devil*, 1513, engraving.

reformers and their opponents, gave rise to a reading public liable to discontent and dissent.

Then as now, works of imagination brought 'time out of joint' into focus by casting murky broad-scale processes into condensed form. One literary creation of particular note appeared anonymously in 1587. Its long-winded title reads, in part, *History of Johannes Faust: The Universally Reviled Sorcerer and Necromancer, How He Signed His Soul Over to the Devil for an Appointed Time, The Strange Adventures He Witnessed and Performed Himself, Until Finally He Received His Due Recompense.* The wordiness represents a symptom of the querulous spirits ghosting abroad.

During the first few decades of the sixteenth century, an astrologer, alchemist and mountebank named George (Jörg, or Georgius) Faust had charmed and scandalized highborn and commoners throughout German lands.[28] The real-life Faust was a charlatan, but he achieved sufficient notoriety to be a legend in his own day. More importantly, the character he inspired enjoyed such fortune as to become, in the words of Ian Watt, one of the 'myths of modern individualism': a restless polymath striving to go beyond the confines of human knowledge.[29]

In the so-called *Faustbuch* the protagonist comes from peasant stock. Native genius and money from a rich uncle enable him to study and obtain a doctorate in divinity. Still dissatisfied, Faust takes up necromancy and conjuration, which put him in touch with Mephostophiles (as the diabolical servant is called here), an infernal agent who promises to serve him for 24 years if he will sign a contract in blood. The scholar agrees and the bargain is sealed. The rest of the book consists of episodes ranging from what are essentially schoolboy pranks to high-flown discussions of theology – plus a tour of Hell. As the Devil's period of service draws to a close, Faust realizes the gravity of his error, but it's too late. He succumbs to melancholy and tells his students not to do as he has done. When the time is up, ghastly sounds are heard from the scholar's chambers. Morning reveals that the Devil has beaten Faust to a pulp, staining the walls with blood and brains; the poor man's eyes and teeth lie scattered on the floor and his broken body crowns a pile of dung.

The *Faustbuch* was written to teach the lesson printed on the frontispiece, below the title: 'Seid Gott unterthenig, widerstehet dem Teuffel, so fleuhet er von euch' ('Submit yourselves to God. Resist the Devil, and he will flee from you' (James 4:7)).[30] The gory conclusion drives home the consequences of disobeying biblical advice. To make his purposes clear, the author appends an injunction to the Preface for 'every Christian to learn . . . to fear God, flee magic, conjuring, and other work of the Devil' in order 'to become eternally blessed in Christ'. After declaring the didactic aims yet again at the end of the book, he closes with a prayer: 'Amen, amen, I wish this for each and every one from the bottom of my heart, AMEN.'

The broad resonance of the Faust story is unthinkable without the backdrop of the Reformation. Tellingly – and like Hamlet – the protagonist studies at Wittenberg. This detail points to Luther and the spirit of contention. For all that, the two figures are not directly equated. Faust may represent a stand-in for the refractory reformer, the 'true face' of Luther. Conversely, Watt argues, the reference can be interpreted to '[effect] a neat polar opposition . . . between Faust and the most famous of Wittenberg's teachers'.[31] From this perspective, the adventurer still embodies 'the dangers of the intellectual professions', but now in contrast to a legitimate theologian.

The fundamental issue leaves no room for confessional hair-splitting. Without a supernatural dimension, human existence is incomplete. Faust is his own man, but as a mortal being he cannot be self-sufficient. His fiendish counterpart does not come looking for him. Faust goes looking for the Devil; he might excel at academic study, but he fails the only test that really matters when he turns away from 'the way, the truth, and the life' (John 14:6).

It did not take long for the *Faustbuch* to appear in English translation. Almost as soon, Christopher Marlowe (1564–1593) composed *The Tragical History of the Life and Death of Doctor Faustus*. Although the title announces a tragedy, the play offers abundant farce, enhancing the high jinks of the *Faustbuch* with the carnivalesque devilry of the medieval stage. The source material benefits from being cast in dramatic form, which brings out the psychological and metaphysical agitation at its core; everything onstage is personal and cosmic at once. Faustus does exactly what other people do, just on a grander scale; his comeuppance proves all the more spectacular for the disproportionate ambition he has shown.

Hell and its functionaries reflect the human world. Mephistophilis cannot fulfil the scholar's wishes until he has received authorization; he occupies a lowly position in the infernal order, like a summoner or bailiff. Lucifer, the chief administrator, barely deigns to interact with the renowned scholar. He only shows up to sign paperwork that Mephistophilis has arranged. As in a medieval allegory – or a modern-day cartoon – a Good Angel and an Evil Angel visit Faustus and offer counsel. The Seven Deadly Sins appear in person to illustrate the stakes of his decision. In keeping with the model of the *Faustbuch*, the play's hero asks for nothing more than what a simpler man might request: 24 years of sport. Diabolical company promises an extended festival season: consorting with beautiful women and powerful men, revelling in luxury and mocking the laws of the earth below and the heavens above.

The academic heirs of Faustus's misadventures disagree about where the play lands in religious debates of the time.[32] On the one hand, events unfold as if to demonstrate the Calvinist argument of predestination. Step by step and point by point, Faustus does everything wrong. One false move leads to the next; ultimately, they pave the way to damnation, sealing a fate written in advance. Alternatively, the drama may be seen to affirm Catholicism. Faustus flouts tradition and hierarchy; his wilfulness calls to mind reformers' heterodox interpretations of the Bible. As in the *Faustbuch*, he strikes the deal with the Devil at Wittenberg and then travels to Italy and Rome to pull assorted stunts, which illustrate the basic sin of scorning the Church, its dogma and its stewards.

It does not matter which side, if any, the playwright took. Marlowe probably sought to promote Christianity in a general, non-committal way in order to find an audience that relished the points of ambiguity he left in the play by accident or design. The 'Epicurism and Atheism' the author is said to have exhibited are also in evidence.[33] Faustus roves about with little regard for anyone but himself, entertaining no ambition other than to have a good time. In this light, one rogue is the alter ego of the other: the author and his creature form two sides of the same coin. While *Doctor Faustus* affirms uncontroversial tenets of belief, between the lines it leaves the possibility for sympathy, and even identification, with its protagonist. Marlowe was overeducated and underemployed – and, it would seem, also a spy.[34] Shortly after writing the play, he died in a tavern brawl.

Literature may serve edifying purposes, but it doesn't have to. What's more, an author may always be dissembling or playing a game. Written for the stage, Marlowe's *Doctor Faustus* exploits the back-and-forth of dialogue and opportunities for spectacle. The truly theatrical aspects of the work derive from the very tricks the Devil is notorious for using: blandishment, seduction and illusion. The bigger the lie, the wilder the ride.

Many voices speak, and not all of them are telling the truth. An atheistic Epicurean can savour points of artful dissonance in this concert. At the outset, the chorus likens Faustus to Icarus, who flew too close to the Sun and plummeted into the sea.[35] The words at the end declare the same:

> Faustus is gone: regard his hellish fall,
> Whose fiendful fortune may exhort the wise,
> Only to wonder at unlawful things,
> Whose deepness doth entice such forward wits
> To practice more than heavenly power permits.[36]

The framing message is unambiguous. No mortal can stay at the cruising altitude of angels – or even devils. An inflated sense of self yields self-destruction. Between these two points, however, many 'songs' are sung as Faustus flies from one adventure to the next. 'The God thou serv'st is thine own appetite,' he says to himself in a lucid moment. Faustus does not lack a conscience; it's just not the strongest component of his being.[37]

In this regard the exceptional individual proves utterly generic. Faustus's self-assessment applies to other, 'real' people of the day. The play's author is just one of them. Vaster and more cynical ambitions met with greater success than Christopher Marlowe ever knew. 'Shall I make spirits fetch me what I please, / Resolve me of all ambiguities, / Perform what desperate enterprise I will?' Faustus muses early in the play.

> I'll have them fly to India for gold,
> Ransack the ocean for orient pearl,
> And search all corners of the new-found world
> For pleasant fruits and princely delicates;
> I'll have them . . .
> Tell the secrets of all foreign kings;
> I'll have them wall all Germany . . .
> . . .
> I'll levy soldiers with the coin they bring . . .
> . . .
> Yea, strange . . . engines for the brunt of war
> . . .
> I'll make my servile spirits to invent.[38]

Outside the theatre, precisely such schemes were in the process of being contrived and executed: colonial ventures, intelligence networks and military operations. Faustus's wishes reflect and repeat those of his contemporaries and predecessors. If they are damnable in his case, they are damnable in general.

Hence the universal implications of a drama centred on one person. More than theological argument, the play offers historical commentary from a diabolical perspective. Devils love human company, especially when people are headstrong and full of pluck. The 'servile spirits' that Faustus would enlist do not really stand under his command, and they ensure his undoing. Have heads of state, merchants and generals made the same mistake?

The peril of modern individualism is less a matter of making the wrong choices than of believing that choice exists where it does not. Faustus thinks himself a free agent who can negotiate advantageous terms of exchange, his soul for worldly benefits. In so doing he shows himself to be a flagrant mediocrity; his trespasses are the stuff of the intervening half-millennium of Christian civilization. Presumably, many other 'great men' have joined him in eternal hellfire.

The Witching Hour of History

The Tragical History of the Life and Death of Doctor Faustus occupies a threshold position between epochs. The exemplary individualist catches sight of the horizon that will define modernity, yet he winds up stuck in the medieval order of the world. The sole mention of Satan in the work underscores the protagonist's predicament. This occurs when the Old Man, one of the play's many allegorical figures, takes the stage.

The first time the Old Man appears, he urges Faustus to 'stay [his] desperate steps' and be mindful of eternal punishment and reward.[39] The second – and last – time the Old Man shows up, he is simply exasperated: 'Accursed Faustus, miserable man, / That from thy soul exclud'st the grace of heaven!'[40] The person Faustus might have grown to be, had he not been so reckless, is on his way out of this world and on to the next life. 'Satan begins to sift me with his pride,' the Old Man declares,

> As in this furnace God shall try my faith,
> My faith, vile hell, shall triumph over thee.
> Ambitious fiends, see how the heavens smile

At your repulse, and laugh your state to scorn!
Hence, hell! for I fly unto my God.

The image of Satan 'sifting' is taken from the New Testament, where it refers to the process of weeding out the damned from the elect.[41] The next line expresses the same idea with a change of emphasis: 'in this furnace God shall try my faith.' On the higher spiritual plane, God and Satan do not stand opposed: the latter separates the wheat from the faithless chaff, which the Lord burns away. The Old Man may face a few unpleasant formalities, but he is confident in the ultimate dispensation of justice. Faustus is too smart to know better.

It is not by chance that a minor magician captured the imagination of so many people during the sixteenth and seventeenth centuries, for the period witnessed what the British historian Hugh Trevor-Roper, in a classic study, denominated the 'European witch craze'.[42] The literary fortunes of Faust took wing when Western Christendom was busy hunting down and rooting out sorcerers and sorceresses. In fact – and in spite of Faust's 'modern' traits (seeking autonomy at any price, defying authority in the name of self-fulfilment and contempt for received pieties) – the *Faustbuch* and Marlowe's play represent the last gasp of the old view of magic, centred on the ostentatious ambitions of a single man. The dawning epoch conceived of magic in other terms: as concerted activity on the part of conspirators, especially female ones, working to overturn true religion and the Christian society built on its foundations.

Medieval culture had set aside room for uncanny knowledge. Mysticism represented a sphere that escaped strict supervision, and what counted as legitimate science was not as defined as it came to be later in history. The educated and uneducated alike acknowledged that there was much the uninitiated could not understand. Practitioners of the occult qualified as objects of official interest insofar as they were perceived as a menace, but this happened rarely. Medieval society had laws against *maleficium* – inflicting harm by magical means – but for centuries legal cases were infrequent (and often handled by secular authorities).[43]

The procedure for bringing charges during the early Middle Ages was the so-called *accusatory*: parties who alleged wrongdoing had to initiate proceedings, and false charges could prove disastrous for those who made them. It was widely believed that people existed who sought to damage others through magic, but the category of someone whose whole life and legal personhood were defined by supernatural agency – a full-blooded witch, as it were – did not really exist. And while frowned upon, witchcraft per se did not represent an activity to evil ends, much less count as an alliance with wicked spirits: assistance might be sought for luck in love, good crops and so forth. Finally, not everyone thought that ritual magic worked – it could simply be the refuge of the deluded and desperate.

The intricacies of the long-term shift in attitudes towards magic exceed what can be described here, but the driving force does not. Prior to the twelfth century, measures to counter beliefs and practices that did not agree with official doctrine were comparatively mild and sporadic. The outlook changed with what has come to be known as the 'Inquisition', writ large.[44] At first an ad-hoc episcopal institution, its methods for rooting out heresy grew more severe as the Church consolidated its teachings and sought to ensure their observance. Hereby, a conception of the Adversary stripped of dialectical nuance took hold.

According to historian Norman Cohn, the persecutory mechanism decisive for the witch trials had come into being centuries earlier in the Church's confrontation with the Waldensians, a group centred in the mountainous region extending from Lyon and the mountains of Switzerland down to Piedmont and Lombardy. This community of believers derived its name from Peter Waldo (Pierre Vaudès, *c.* 1140–*c.* 1218), a wealthy merchant who gave away his possessions, embraced poverty and sought to renew primitive religious virtue through predication. Similar movements had existed before, but circumstances now dictated a stern view (especially given the perceived vigour of so-called Catharism, a dualist strain of Christianity that flourished in neighbouring areas to the southwest).[45] In order to combat dissent, a 'new kind of trial' with a novel mode of operation was established.[46] By 'inquisitorial procedure', authorities secular or ecclesiastical set up autonomous investigations that no longer relied on specific charges made by individuals who thought they had been wronged personally. The field stood open for sniffing out and hunting down fractious elements.

Still, relative moderation prevailed for centuries. Witch trials occurred in the late Middle Ages, but inasmuch as they focused on powerful (or, at any rate, influential) individuals, their scope was limited. Hell broke loose during the age of religious wars (broadly speaking, the sixteenth and seventeenth centuries). Under conditions of institutional and political contention between Christians, deviant activities were thought to betoken false *allegiance*, not backwardness or superstition.

Medieval folklore about witchcraft had not included pacts with the Devil. Spirits good and bad were supposed to further the aims of those who appealed to them, of course, but such powers did not constitute a chartered body. The nightmarish vision of a diabolical league arose only when learned men in the Church tried to systematize heteroclite beliefs and practices among rural folk, idiosyncratic autodidacts and assorted regional movements. Phenomena that would have remained isolated came together in an interpretive scheme that presumed coherence where none existed. The leader of the putative host working against Christian unity could only be Satan. What previously might have been dismissed as idle falsehood and delusion came to suggest an active campaign of lies and malice.

An expanded and instrumentalized understanding of heresy justified inquisitorial practice. The concept had emerged some thousand years earlier. Etymologically, the Greek word *hairesis* is related to acts of will, or 'self-chosen opinion'. In the New Testament Epistles it means something along the lines of 'sect'.[47] In the second century Irenaeus, Bishop of Lugdunum in Gaul (modern-day Lyon, France), put the term into broader circulation while polemicizing against Christians who did not adhere to the doctrines of the Church:

> Let those . . . who blaspheme the Creator, whether openly, or [covertly] . . . be recognized as agents of Satan by all who worship God – those through whose agency Satan now has been seen to speak against God, who has prepared eternal fire for every kind of apostasy.[48]

Thinking and speaking the wrong thing in the eyes of the Lord (or, more precisely, His earthly representatives) does not qualify as an accident or mistake; it amounts to a conscious decision to side with the Adversary. The latter is not 'the satan' of the Old and New Testaments so much as the mythical embodiment of evil. As defiance of the Lord, heresy merits the gravest punishment. That said, Irenaeus did not prescribe immediate action; God would do as He saw fit. For centuries to come, the Church proved more welcoming and syncretic than exclusionary, without internal agreement or sufficient power to enforce rules outwardly.

Following the Reformation, the idea of an organized body of enemies in Europe obtained real plausibility. Islam counted as a threat to religious and political cohesion only at the borderlands. By the end of the fifteenth century the *Reconquista* of the Iberian Peninsula was complete; there were no Muslims left. The menace continued at the eastern border of Europe, but inasmuch as relations were overtly hostile, there was no mistaking 'us' and 'them'. Jews, who were more numerous, fitted the criteria for persecution much better.[49] Many of the latter entertained regular (if uneasy) contact with Gentile neighbours; a few even rose to positions of wealth and prominence. Terrible pogroms occurred in the Middle Ages, to be sure, but officially Rome urged toleration of a people once favoured by God. The indignities that Jews endured counted as punishment enough for their 'errors', and the fact that Judaism is not a proselytizing religion minimized the prospect of subversive influence.[50]

The situation of Christians – or people who were supposed to be Christians – was different. They stood to lose privileges and rights if they fell under suspicion of rejecting the faith. Then, the same powers guaranteeing their safety might seek their destruction. Cohn puts the process in psychoanalytic terms: inquisitors took 'ancient legends' and confessions obtained under torture from 'neurotic or sexually frustrated' individuals as confirmation that a confederacy sworn to evil powers existed.[51] In this context dreams about supernatural flights and diabolical encounters counted as evidence that the accused had yielded to Satan spiritually, if not physically.[52] Accounts of gatherings that perverted holy ritual and witnessed human intercourse with demons commanded particular attention. Authorities '[lent] an ear to popular complaints about *maleficium*',[53] which previously they would have brushed aside as superstition or resentful calumny.

'The role of the demonic associate [underwent] a radical change': instead of being imagined as a servant, he was pictured as a master.[54] Relative nobodies like Mephistophilis gave way to Lucifer. Whereas *maleficia* had previously been deemed a means of settling scores on a petty level, now a worldwide secret society of heretical sorcerers came into view. And because witchcraft was thought to be a global phenomenon, the most important thing, after obtaining the accused's confession, was to learn the names of other witches.

In other words, the witch craze occurred from the top down:

Left to themselves, peasants would never have created mass witch-hunts – these occurred only where and when the authorities had become convinced of the reality of the sabbat and of nocturnal flights to the sabbat. And this conviction depended on, and in turn was sustained by, the inquisitorial type of procedure, including the use of torture. When suspected witches could be compelled . . . to name those whom they had seen at the sabbat, all things became possible: the mayor and town councilors and their wives were just as likely to be accused as were peasant women.[55]

Witch-hunters started from the assumption that folk beliefs and neighbourhood rumours amounted to more than rustic humbug

The grandeur and abjection of witchcraft: Andries Jacobsz Stock, after Jacques de Gheyn II, *Witches' Sabbath*, c. 1610, engraving.

and ill-will: those who practised magic in an 'amateur' capacity were actually up to something far more sinister. Once officials acted on this theory, they found ample evidence in lore that had existed for ages and confessions obtained by force. The mechanism of persecution then functioned on its own, recoding popular fears and enmities in terms of a single stereotype.

The witch craze gripped Western Christendom as a whole: Satan, the ancient accuser, might be thought to have convinced rival factions to eliminate his supposed agents. Inquisitorial efforts by Catholics were matched by campaigns undertaken by Protestants.[56] Both sides faced the same peril: dissolution from within. Both exhibited the same fervour in ferreting out disloyal elements potentially in league with external enemies. Self-righteous violence was ecumenical. Failing to pass the Adversary's test of Christian compassion, the witch-hunters exposed their own desire for their co-religionists' blood.

Satanic Synopsis

The Middle Ages might have been backward and superstitious, but the Age of Reformation fomented paranoia and persecution.[57] If medieval dogma held that the human heart is sinful, early modern times rediscovered the mind's boundless perversity. Satan, whether real or imagined, moved from the bowels of the earth into the haunted, chattering skulls of mortals with only a defective conscience to guide them.

Now, the Adversary did a great deal of talking. Depending on the source, he was whispering to the papacy, Protestant upstarts or the jumbled and confused 'conspiracy' of witches. Across the spectrum, early modern Christians acknowledged the key role that the Devil, sometimes assisted by lesser devils, plays in historical events. Catholics and Reformers could devise equally compelling arguments – and enlist equally many men at arms – to combat rivals while claiming the mantle of holiness for themselves. More than ever, Satan was busy 'going to and fro in the earth', making trial of credulous mortals who were mustering troops and erecting tribunals to kill each other in the name of the Lord.

FIVE

The Devil's Party

Christianity overtook both Judaism, of which it was born, and the cults of the Hellenistic-Roman world. The Gospels of Matthew, Mark and Luke use the parable of the mustard seed to illustrate the Kingdom of God flourishing over the earth. History yields a different picture. When the seed took root on a wide range of soils in varied climates, so did the weeds of heresy. Another biblical metaphor presents the faithful as ruminants roaming from one place to the next and chewing their cud. But flocks do not always follow shepherds, and the bell-wethers appointed to lead them have been castrated. In the material world, inhospitable terrain, intermittent starvation and contests for power are a given.

Religion is not really a plant. The human animal is not really a sheep. One and a half millennia after the Saviour walked the earth, Thomas Hobbes (1588–1679) contemplated the state of Christendom as a whole and the events of the English Civil War (1642–51) in particular. The spectacle prompted him to revisit pagan wisdom. *Homo homini lupus*, 'man is a wolf to man.'[1] Medieval theology had posited a hierarchical arrangement for nature and society, as per providential design. Hobbes reversed the perspective, made brute reality the starting point and named two of his treatises on government after Old Testament monsters: *Leviathan* (1651) and *Behemoth* (written in 1668; published 1681). Although civilization takes on terrifying forms, it is still better than the state of nature, which amounts to *bellum omnium contra omnes*, 'a war of all against all'.

Unappreciative contemporaries accused Hobbes of atheism. In fact, he was playing the Devil's advocate by stressing *motion*. Open-ended processes, not immutable structures, shape the world.[2] Such an outlook does not deny the existence of the Deity. If God has seen fit to be absent for a spell, the empty space where *He is not* highlights divine transcendence. Mortals teem and wither, grow and die. The Lord, whose infinite domain admits understanding only in negative terms, suffers no constraints in time or space.

This chapter explores Satan and his associates as planners and schemers in a busy universe. The first part examines the most ambitious representation of the Adversary to date, John Milton's *Paradise Lost* (1664). Milton's charismatic Devil tries to induce the archetypal human beings, Adam and Eve, to follow him into dissipation. Protestant drive sets this Satan apart from the creaky executor of medieval justice in Dante's *Inferno*.

The second part revisits the Faust legend. Johann Wolfgang von Goethe's protagonist achieves heights the Reformation-era Faustus could never have imagined, but the scholar's diabolical counterpart shows him that this means sinking to matching depths. In contrast to Milton's Satan, Goethe's Devil knows he is full of hot air. As ever, the Adversary administers a trial, but now he challenges the restless individualist to catch up with his own desires. Faust crashes all the more dramatically for having soared on infernal wings.

Finally, we turn to the Romantic poets, for whom Satan pleads the case of the dispossessed. Meek no more and ready to inherit the earth, the abject masses rally around a lost cause. In their rush for rewards promised but never delivered by a seemingly derelict Deity, they fall for an infernal ruse. Satan is testing the desperate not to follow their dreams.

Free Speech and Free Fall

At each stage of life, John Milton (1608–1674) displayed a combative spirit.[3] An altercation with his tutor prompted his dismissal from university study. Later, when the rule of Charles I (1600–1649) faltered, Milton sharpened his pen for the republican cause and made a name for himself defending divorce, attacking clerical norms and even advocating regicide. After the Commonwealth was established, such opinions no longer counted as treasonous; under Oliver Cromwell, the erstwhile rebel became 'Secretary for Foreign Tongues'. But in 1660 the monarchy returned. A warrant was issued demanding Milton's arrest, his screeds were burned and he went into hiding. From obscurity – and long since blind – he published the first edition of *Paradise Lost* in 1664.

Paradise Lost 'pursues / Things unattempted yet in Prose or Rhyme' in order to 'assert Eternal Providence / And justify the ways of God to men'.[4] The task is far from straightforward; it calls for representing things that elude mortal grasp in terms comprehensible to finite minds. Accounts for the world's origins and divine purposes are as old as civilization itself, but Milton's poem must 'justify' an arrangement harbouring flaws in monotheistic terms. Why did God, who is omniscient and omnipotent, see fit to allow for a vitiated creature such as 'man' in the first place?

Milton appreciates that his 'adventurous Song' represents a fraught endeavour, and he invokes a 'Heavenly Muse' for assistance.[5] This guide, the poet declares, has a seat 'on the secret top / of *Oreb*, or of *Sinai*', not Parnassus or Helicon.[6] Still, a muse is a muse; the word evokes the goddesses of song in classical antiquity, which knew nothing of the Lord. At least in part, *Paradise Lost* is woven from strands of pagan eloquence. What's more, the epic tradition celebrates war, not peace; discord and strife give rise to mighty deeds by parties who are imposing, but not necessarily good in a moral sense (like the biblical giants, or 'men of renown'[7]). Its substance derives more from heathen feats of strength than from Christian humility.

Samuel Ireland, after Charles Townley and William Hogarth, *Satan, Sin and Death*, 1788, etching and engraving for John Milton's *Paradise Lost*, Book II.

William Blake (1757–1827) would later observe that Milton 'wrote in fetters . . . of Angels and God, and at liberty . . . of Devils and Hell'.[8] The path of righteousness is narrow – and often dull. Evil demonstrates boundless invention, in spite of the fact that its failure has been foreordained. If only in formal terms, 'th'Arch-Enemy' plays the main role for much of what Milton committed to the page;[9] even fiction in service to religion demands engaging characters and plot. The 'great Argument' presented in *Paradise Lost* stands in conflict with the eventful narration, which overflows with deceptive schemes that provoke perverse wonder.[10] Art, verbal or otherwise, will bend moral codes as it seeks to rouse sentiment and stimulate the mind. It is more than possible that Milton was 'of the Devil's party without knowing it'.[11]

Paradise Lost begins, then, with a question that the rest of the poem may or may not answer to one's satisfaction.

> Say first, for Heaven hides nothing from thy view,
> Nor the deep Tract of Hell, say first what cause
> Mov'd our Grand Parents, in that happy State,
> Favour'd of Heaven so highly, to fall off
> From their Creator, and transgress his Will
> For one restraint, lords of the World besides?
> Who first seduced them to that foul revolt?[12]

On the surface, the answer seems easy enough. Adam and Eve were 'mov'd' to 'fall off / From their Creator' because the Devil made them do it: 'Th'infernal Serpent; he it was.'[13] That said, humankind's 'Grand Parents' already face trouble in their 'happy State'. For reasons they cannot know, God has allowed for error as part of intelligent design, and his creatures need to exercise divinely granted faculties in the right way. The provision that has placed human beings at the summit of Creation is not just a blessing, but a curse. Bodily senses, and the reason that crowns them, must be employed judiciously. When Adam and Eve fail to do so, their 'foul revolt' appears fair.

Satan soon shows up to point them in the wrong direction. Before that, afterwards and throughout much of the poem, he steals the show. He's just too entertaining.

Although bruised from being 'hurl'd headlong flaming' into 'bottomless perdition', 'great *Lucifer*' looks and sounds mighty – godlike, even – at the antipode of the Empyrean heights.[14] When he has composed himself sufficiently, 'th'Apostate Angel' launches into mile-a-minute oratory.[15] Appealing to his companions as 'natives and sons of Heaven', he asks a question of his own:

> Will ye submit your necks, and choose to bend
> The supple knee? ye will not, if I trust
> To know ye right, or if ye know yourselves . . .
>
> . . .
>
> Who can in reason . . . or right assume
> Monarchy over such as live by right
> His equals . . . ?[16]

Boisterous words and riotous deeds all but derail the poet's pious yet plodding exposition of the theology of salvation.

Satan's 'Peers' rally to the cause of the infernal commonwealth, intent on renewing 'War in Heaven and Battel proud' from below.[17] It would seem that the irony of the Devil delivering an impassioned republican declamation escaped the real-life author of his speech. Then again, Satan's foremost resource is not being what he seems to be. The Adversary projects authority and shows winning ways to his own kind, in whose eyes he radiates the same perfection he once possessed as a member of the heavenly court.

Devils live in intellectual and moral error; they see, hear and think according to rules governing a realm in which 'self-chosen opinion' – heresy – amounts to physical reality. 'Affecting . . . equality with God',[18] the grandstanding speaker enjoins his listeners to do the same. When Satan employs philosophical language ('know yourselves') and calls on his audience's sense of 'reason' and 'right', he is spouting sophistry. No basis exists for wise judgement among the infernal host. Consequently, the audience is thrilled to hear that God the Father acted as a tyrant by imposing 'Law and Edict on us, who without law / Err not'.[19] The same holds for the claim that God the Son has 'us eclipst under the name / Of King anointed',[20] usurped rights that should be shared and introduced ranks and distinctions where before there were none.

Paradise Lost is not known for its humour, yet the abyss separating lofty ambitions from lowly conditions can be pretty funny. Satan's sloganeering is cast in concrete form in the 'high Capitol' of Hell, Pandaemonium.[21] Though exquisitely crafted, it occupies a tiny space; the diabolical hordes must shrink down to minuscule dimensions to take up residence there. Hell and its mansions are as great and, ultimately, as petty as its denizens. The time it takes for the infernal city to be built is equally remarkable. It shoots up in less than a day – which would be a miracle if the whole undertaking weren't a mirage. The residence of Leviathan, Behemoth and the rest of the gang rests on a foundation of smoke and mirrors.

The Satanic state strives for a backwards-looking ideal that never was. Any real duration or substance depends on realizing its leader's plan to infiltrate the weakest point in God's Kingdom and, from there, topple the Heavenly Throne. Hoping to secure an outpost and win recruits, Satan takes aim for the 'blissful Bower' made by the 'sovran Planter' for Adam and 'his fair Spouse'.[22] Painful hilarity ensues.

The Protestant universe is vast and full of uncharted terrain; despite his big talk, the Adversary must go it alone. His voyage across the waves separating the cosmic continents unfolds as one-man slapstick. Instead of resembling the grand voyages of pre-Christian epic, Satan's journey seems like the clumsy manoeuvring of a cartoon character – more Wile E. Coyote than Odysseus or Aeneas. 'The Fiend' makes his way only with immense effort:

> At last his Sail-broad Vans
> He spreads for flight, and in the surging smoke
> Uplifted spurns the ground, thence many a League
> As in a cloudy Chair ascending rides
> Audacious, but, that seat soon failing, meets
> A vast vacuity: all unawares
> Flutt'ring his pennons vain plumb-down he drops
> Ten thousand fathom deep, and to this hour
> Down had been falling, had not by ill chance
> The strong rebuff of some tumultuous cloud
> Instinct with Fire and Nitre hurried him
> As many miles aloft.[23]

Satan can barely navigate the elements between the landmasses of the universe. 'Nigh founder'd on he fares, / Treading the crude consistence, half on foot, / Half flying'; 'with head, hands, wings, or feet', he 'pursues his way, / And swims or sinks, or wades, or creeps, or flies'.[24] Only in Hell, among his vanquished brethren, does he retain his former majesty: when he takes stumbling flight, he has difficulty even keeping his footing.

After a seeming eternity of spastic motion, Satan reaches *terra firma.* Here he appears in a different light. The Adversary still displays supernatural powers of movement and metamorphosis, yet they prove undignified as he, now a poisonous buffoon, wheedles and connives. Although matters are grave, they possess an absurd quality. The tragedy of the Fall from the Palace of Heaven repeats itself as a farce in the Garden of Eden.

On solid ground, Satan cannot stand proud. 'Squat like a Toad, close at the ear of *Eve*', he whispers sweet talk,

> Assaying by his Devilish art to reach
> The Organs of her Fancy, and with them forge
> Illusions as he list, Phantasms and Dreams;
> Or if, inspiring venom, he might taint
> Th'animal spirits, that from pure blood arise
> Like gentle breaths from Rivers pure, thence raise
> At least distemper'd, discontented thoughts,
> Vain hopes, vain aims, inordinate desires
> Blown up with high conceits ingend'ring pride.[25]

As before, Satan traffics in lies: 'Illusions . . . Phantasms and Dreams'. He cannot offer anything of substance, and so his gifts are pitted and hollow. At the same time, these verbal trinkets spread unreality and pollute those with whom they come into contact. The soil of human being lies fallow; Satan plants seeds of discontent, 'taint[ing] / Th'animal spirits that from pure blood arise'.

Instead of grazing on the fruits that grow from uncorrupted being, Adam and Eve reach to nibble at 'vain hopes, vain aims,

'Towards the coast of Earth beneath, / Down from the ecliptic, sped with hoped success, / Throws his steep flight in many an aery wheel.' Illustration by Gustave Doré for John Milton's *Paradise Lost*, Book III (1866 edn).

[and] inordinate desires' just out of reach. Before Cain and Abel were born and one brother killed the other, fatal 'pride' was born of the void that is both Satan's element and his infectious offering. Hence the famous line that God has made Man 'sufficient to have stood' yet 'free to fall'.[26] However clownish he looks and acts, Satan is still the tester.

For Protestants in general, but especially for Puritans, human beings are their own worst enemies. Adam and Eve must answer for their sin; even though there are mitigating circumstances, and God is inclined to show them mercy, they need not have yielded to the temptation they bred within. *Paradise Lost* makes Satan the bad guy, but it also exempts him from blame once his provocation is complete.

Milton takes up parts of Genesis and the Book of Revelation, the story of Eden and the vision of War in Heaven. These episodes belong to biblical 'prehistory': the first is a creation myth that stands apart from everything else in the Tanakh, and the second, which barely made it into the canon at all, concerns a time before the material world came into being. The rest of the Bible, which constitutes the substance of Judaism and Christianity (the Patriarchs, passage from Egypt to the Promised Land, the Sermon on the Mount, the Last Supper, the Crucifixion), does not really enter the picture. The whole of *Paradise Lost* – a series of 'high conceits' with tenuous scriptural support – is impressive, but its spirit belongs to the poet's own day. If Milton's work has not been consigned to oblivion, it is because the Adversary and his plans, ridiculous and sublime in equal measure, still enchant inhabitants of 'this transient World'.[27]

Whatever else may be said of him, Milton's villain has principles. 'Better to reign in Hell than serve in Heaven', he famously declares.[28] Even if his project produces a mess, its author wants *something*. Satan in *Paradise Lost* exhibits qualities his medieval forerunner lacked: personality, wit and will – plus a political agenda. The 'Devil's party' promises 'liberty', even if the enterprise proves to be self-defeating.

Up in Smoke, Down the Drain

But what if the Adversary stood for nothing at all? Goethe's *Faust* explores this possibility, giving him licence to make a mockery of the modern individualist who dreams that his dull life will yet yield 'adventurous Song'. Early modern treatments of the material, some two hundred years earlier, still rested on medieval cosmology. Marlowe's Faustus, like the infernal brood he consorts with, belongs to the created universe. The ill-starred hero's horizons do not reach beyond the earth; indeed, as the parade of the Seven Deadly Sins makes clear, they barely extend beyond his physical appetites. In contrast, Goethe's Faust seeks to leave all he knows behind, and with it the pettiness of human existence in general. The work opens onto a different vista: the unrestricted – and aimless – pursuit of fulfilment at once personal and impersonal, a kind of atheistic communion.

A 'Prologue in Heaven' precedes the drama. Raphael, Gabriel, Michael and Mephistopheles – the 'odd man out' in the heavenly host – approach the Lord to report on the state of Creation. The first three angels describe its wonders and glory. The fourth paints a dreary picture, remarking on humankind's toils and troubles. To the extent that Mephistopheles can bring himself to care for mortals' plight, he feels only pity. The earth offers 'a rather sorry sight'.[29] God, benevolent but detached, asks Mephistopheles whether he has encountered 'my servant', Faust.[30] The Lord is optimistic that this man's life, even if it follows an idiosyncratic course, will ultimately affirm that all is right with the world that He has made. The Devil begs to differ, and the 'bet' is on.[31] Goethe presents his work as a new Book of Job. Unlike his forebear, Faust is no model of piety or duty, whatever the distracted Deity might say.

The perilous adventure of learning: Rembrandt van Rijn, *A Scholar in His Study (Faust)*, 1650–54, etching on paper.

Before Mephistopheles appears to him, the scholar takes the stage and delivers his famous lament, *Habe nun, ach!*[32] – a summary dismissal of human learning. Seeing the nullity of others' efforts and the vanity of his own pursuits, he decides to turn to magic. Faust casts aside scholastic treatises and opens a mystical tome. He exclaims:

> What jubilation bursts out of this sight
> Into my senses – now I feel it flowing,
> Youthful, a sacred fountain of delight,
> Through every nerve, my veins are glowing.

A new dimension seems to unfold. Faust asks, 'Am I a god? Light grows so bright!'[33] Needless to say, he is not. Faust welcomes an invigorating surge of excitation – the kind that might be produced, on a more modest scale, by a pinch of snuff, cup of coffee or any other stimulant. His references to 'senses', 'nerves' and 'veins' reveal his transport to be more physical than metaphysical in kind. The scholar does not seek insight so much as a life he thinks he has been missing. After the passing exhilaration has worn off, he exclaims:

> What play! Yet but a play, however vast!
> Where, boundless nature, can I hold you fast?[34]

Faust's appetite is for 'boundless nature'. Certainly, this is too much for any one man to wish for, much less hold fast.

All the same, the protagonist tries to cling to the tide that washes over him. Still mildly 'high', but not high enough, Faust beholds the magic sign for summoning another elemental spirit and rhapsodizes:

> How different is the power of this sign!
> You, spirit of the earth, seem close to mine:

> I look and feel my powers growing,
> As if I'd drunk new wine I'm glowing.[35]

This expedient does not last long, either. Faust lapses back into the sullen mood that preceded his short-lived magical flight. Finally, in despair, he resolves to quaff a potion stronger than wine: the 'essence of slumber-bringing juices'.[36] Poison will put an end to his impossible quest by sending him on the ultimate trip: death. Life in general is tedious, and the life of the mind is just an exercise in frustration. Faust stands as a representative of modern mythology not just because of his appetite for mind-altering substances, but because he exhibits what would now be called bipolar disorder.[37]

Like the *Faustbuch* and Marlowe's *Tragical History*, Goethe's play does not present a favourable portrait of the scholar. Although he has reached the pinnacle of learning, Faust remains dissatisfied, for none of the academic disciplines has revealed how to make sense of a pointless existence. Thus when the Devil comes to him, he does so as 'the spirit that always negates' – the form that befits *action*, not contemplation.[38] The paradox at the heart of the work is that self-affirmation amounts to self-loss. Faust expresses no concern for insight or truth; he only opens a book to supply a jolt to his enervated mortal frame. The immediate bodily effect from what he ingests, observes or otherwise takes in interests him more than the wisdom to which it might lead. Faust seeks a life of consumption. He does not want to get behind appearances so much as he wants to be surrounded by them and lose himself in them.

Faust does not get anything at all for signing a contract with the Adversary. The first part of the drama takes place immediately before Easter. While simpler souls celebrate the rebirth promised through Christ, Faust is scouring dusty spell books and trying, in vain, to rekindle vital force. When Mephistopheles appears, Faust takes up with him without a second thought. At the end of his proverbial rope and devoid of all faith in this world and the next, the scholar feels he has nothing to lose. The Devil, who traffics in illusions, need hardly lift a finger; Faust is ready to go.

Because he sets his own terms, Faust strikes a fool's bargain. All he asks for is nervous stimulation:

> The reeling whirl I seek, the most painful excess,
> Enamored hate and quickening distress.
> Cured from the craving to know all, my mind
> Shall not henceforth be closed to any pain,
> And what is portioned out to all mankind,
> I shall enjoy deep in myself.[39]

Faust demands constant excitement. Painful excess, enamoured hate and quickening distress can all be experienced without enlisting infernal assistance. What Goethe's hero is looking for is already 'portioned out to all mankind'; he just wants an extra dose. Faust, like many others in this world, is unhappy about his limitations. Like a good number of them, he seeks to remedy the situation by taking a shortcut. In the language of substance abuse counselling, Mephistopheles is an 'enabler'.

The real tragedy, then, does not concern Faust so much as the person unlucky enough to fall into his company. The first place Mephistopheles takes the thrill-seeking academic is a tavern. The hero tries to join the revel but soon learns that the potations enjoyed by the salt of the earth will not do the trick. Mephistopheles then conducts Faust to a witch's kitchen, where he imbibes stronger stuff. With a 'potion's aid', the scholar looks through a magic mirror and finds himself enchanted by the idealized feminine image he beholds.[40] This is not love. The witch's brew affects Faust's nerves more than his heart or even his loins, making him indulge in vacuous fantasy. Gretchen is a nice girl, but hardly anything special (at least by her own account). When Faust's eye fastens on her, her fate is sealed: even if he does so unwittingly, he will use and abuse her until she is consumed entirely to feed his empty transports. An intoxicant commandeers everything – including eros.

Lest there be any doubt, the play culminates in the extended hallucination of Walpurgis Night. Like a drug fiend stuporously chasing after his next fix, Faust follows a will-o'-the-wisp to the Witches' Sabbath; his secret sharer Mephistopheles also comes along. The three travellers sing a song on their merry way: their voices are indistinguishable.

> In the sphere of dream and spell
> We have entered now indeed.
> Have some pride and guide us well
> That we get ahead with speed
> In the vast deserted spaces![41]

Since the text does not assign parts to distinct characters, Faust might as well be dreaming it all up. He remains alone, even in company. The question he voices goes unanswered:

> Tell me: do we now stand still,
> Or do we go up the hill?
> Everything now seems to mill,

> Rocks and trees and faces blend,
> Will-o'-the-wisps grow and extend
> And inflate themselves at will.[42]

The will-o'-the-wisp then dissolves into the lapping waves of deceptive phenomena, as does Mephistopheles. Faust, who does not belong here, rises and falls in the shadows of a chaotic realm without reference or stability. By now any power of discernment he might have possessed has vanished. He has long lost any moral bearings he might have had, too.

The host with which Faust consorts on the sabbath could just as well be sprung from his own addled mind, fed by decades of reading and contempt for the everyday world he has never been able to join. In a whirling gyre, mythological entities, witches in chorus and a parade of grotesque social types appear: participants in a carnival parodying the holy setting of the drama as a whole. Easter, without the miracle of resurrection, is a pagan free-for-all, a feast for the senses. The excitement makes the learned man, who is either out of his mind or lost in an inner labyrinth, question the one true image he beholds:

> Mephisto, do you see
> That pale, beautiful child, alone there on the heather?
> She moves slowly but steadily,
> She seems to walk with her feet chained together.
> I must confess that she, forbid,
> Looks much as my poor Gretchen did.[43]

The Devil, in turn, steers him back to the party: 'That does nobody good; leave it alone! / It is a magic image, a lifeless apparition.'[44]

Devils must spark interest for their powers to work: Jan Luyken, 'Woman Walks Quietly Past Satan', illustration in *Voncken der liefde Jesu* (Sparks of the Love of Jesus, 1687).

Giving himself over to the visions once more, Faust forgets all about Gretchen. When he wakes up with a hellish hangover,[45] it is too late to save her. Overdosed on love for her undeserving paramour, she has gone mad and drowned the child she conceived with him. Now she faces execution.

Mephistopheles practically disappears in the protagonist's debauched sport. His sinister-sounding name suggests far greater ill than he incarnates or causes. True to his matter-of-fact, amoral nature, Mephistopheles toys with his victim, but without malice: 'I feel as does the cat about the mouse.'[46] Indeed, he displays a certain world-weary wisdom. If this Devil has any point to prove, it's that the world is neither good nor bad, and even the wisest man is a fool. Mephistopheles is the only member of the heavenly host to have observed just how tiresome affairs are on earth, and he alone recognizes the vanity of Faust's every presumption.

As in the Hebrew Bible, this 'satan' tests the man who has found favour in the eyes of the Lord. But at the dawn of the modern age, God's favourite – and maybe God Himself – is found wanting. Goethe's Mephistopheles is Milton's Adversary, minus the scheming and ambition: a nonentity. His games of illusion teach a lesson few of Faust's countless real-world counterparts, intent on taking life by the horns, have been inclined to heed: 'Don't even try.' The libertarian scholar wishes to make a fresh start; his 'servant' winds up running the show.

Titanic Effort and Insincere Repentance

Something devilish attended the evolution of modern literature: a combination of thrill-seeking, insubordination and identification with the outcast. The embodiment of this spirit, which Mario Praz denominated 'the Romantic agony', was the internationally notorious George Gordon, Lord Byron (1788–1824), whose profligate life mirrored his scandalous verse.[47] When Robert Southey (1774–1843) denounced Byron and his friend Percy Bysshe Shelley for founding 'the Satanic School' of letters,[48] the publicity-loving author proudly made the title his own. Thanks to his bold words, adventurous existence and death at a young age, the author of *The Corsair* and *Don Juan* offered the model for the outsiders of nineteenth-century literature and legend, from gloomily charismatic loners in the novels of the Brontë sisters to the personae adopted by French *poètes maudits* a few decades later.

Like all Satanism, Byron's romance with the dark side displays a religious quality, however confused. When the world is reeling madly, a toss of the coin may prove as reliable as a purposeful decision. And if right and wrong harmonize in some mysterious way, 'bad' is not 'evil'; indeed, bad may lead to good. *Motion* – dynamism and change – is what counts.

Byron's poem 'Prometheus' (1816), which glorifies the titan condemned to eternal torment for having given mortals fire in defiance of the will of Zeus, expresses the pathos of such endeavour.

> Thy Godlike crime was to be kind,
> To render with thy precepts less
> The sum of human wretchedness,
> And strengthen Man with his own mind . . .[49]

By Byron's account, the mythological rebel almost seems to be a figure for the Christian redeemer. The word 'Godlike' marks a fundamental difference, however. Prometheus shows himself to be *like* God (or the gods), but not on the same plane. In a Judeo-Christian framework, the hero's name would have to be Lucifer, 'Bearer of Light'. He may well offer 'a symbol and a sign / To mortals of their fate and force',[50] but *fate* carries more weight.

Goethe looked down on Byron and his peers, but even at Olympian heights he belonged to his age. The lion of German

The Promethean idol: Mathieu Barathier, *The Apotheosis of Lord Byron*, 1826, lithograph.

letters lived a long life, from 1749 to 1832. Reinhart Koselleck has dubbed roughly the same stretch of time the 'saddle period' (*Sattelzeit*) of European history.[51] In geology, 'saddle' designates the area hemmed in by peaks; for Koselleck, it refers to the temporal and cultural expanse between epochs displaying greater definition in abstract, if not concrete, terms. Up to 1750 the Old Regime sat firm inasmuch as positions of power could be contested, but not the overall organization of society or structures of rule. After about 1850 another system was ascendant: now, representative government, liberalized economic policies, guarantees of religious freedom and so on came to stand as the norm in theory, if not in practice. The author of *Faust* witnessed, commented on and participated in the great events of the day; the protagonist of his masterpiece embodies the *Zeitgeist* and all its contradictions.[52]

Heinrich Heine (1797–1856) jokingly called Goethe 'the great pagan' of German culture.[53] This poet, who had a diabolical streak of his own, knew what he was talking about. Like Goethe's Mephistopheles, Heine took a dim view of human affairs and reckoned there was nothing better to come. Life is already hell – why not try to make at least part of it an earthly paradise? In his own version of the Faust story, 'Mephistophela' teaches the world-weary scholar how to dance.[54]

Jewish by birth, Heine converted to Protestantism to avoid the professional disadvantages that his heritage entailed. He did not take religious tradition or dogma of any stripe seriously and viewed politics with the same irreverence. More or less everything the poet wrote displays the *sprezzatura* of a courtier from another time transplanted into the nineteenth-century metropolis. Hence the hints of Satanic melancholy between bursts of wit:

> I called the Devil and he came,
> His face with wonder I must scan;
> He is not ugly, he is not lame,
> He is a delightful, charming man;
> A man in the prime of life, in fact,
> Courteous, engaging, and full of tact.

> A diplomat, too, of wide research
> Who cleverly talks about State and Church.[55]

Heine points out just how readily the Adversary appears when summoned – not to bargain for souls or to contrive anyone's doom, but simply to banter about the generally deplorable condition of humanity. Displaying the qualities of a 'delightful, charming man' – and 'courteous, engaging, and full of tact', too – the Devil exhibits distinction. In the age of mass movements, mass culture and mass politics, standing out from the crowd seems positively other-worldly. (Lest we forget, 'the satan' of the Hebrew Bible numbers among the sons of God.) For Heine, Satan belongs to this world. Like the poet who entertains him – and whom he entertains in turn – he commentates earthly affairs; he is no more evil than his interlocutor or the goings-on they discuss.

Intimacy with the Devil marks either a new state of affairs or a very old one. What if Satan's scintillating dejection represented a dressed-up version of the miserable existence endured by millions upon millions of people? Capitalism may have heightened such alienation – as Heine's contemporary and friend Karl Marx (1818–1883) averred – but the Book of Genesis already made the first human beings unwelcome in the world.

Many others in Heine's day – and afterwards, too – confessed to social intercourse with infernal elements. *Le Diable à Paris*, which appeared in two volumes in 1845 and 1846, presents the 'mores and customs, characters and portraits' of the great city's 'inhabitants'.[56] The collection brought together essays, short stories and engravings by authors and artists of note (including Honoré de Balzac, J. J. Grandville, Alfred de Musset, Gérard de Nerval and George Sand). The conceit was to offer episodes of interest to a visitor from Hell. Like any tourist guide, it pointed out attractions a foreigner would appreciate. Coming to Paris from Pandaemonium, underworld spirits would feel right at home in both palaces and slums.

With much more gravity and religious sentiment, Charles Baudelaire (1821–1867) declared as much, too. While committed to classical form and tradition, Baudelaire sought to be 'the painter of modern life',[57] bringing forth a body of work as appalling as it is beautiful. Cultivated in the cracks and gutters of Paris, *The Flowers of Evil* (1857) depicts dealings in back alleys and brothels with a relish for grotesque detail comparable to paintings by the Dutch masters centuries earlier. For this morbid Roman Catholic voluptuary, misery and crime renew the timeless drama of the human soul, striving to soar but mired in filth. Baudelaire knew that judgement had been pronounced on high, even if it seemed long in coming. In the meanwhile, falling sidelong into the tide of sin and strife, he lived to make a virtue of vice.[58]

Addressing his reader as a fellow 'hypocrite',[59] Baudelaire points to lineaments of abiding truth behind the intoxicating – and nauseating – surge of metropolitan crowds. Like a photographic negative, Baudelaire's 'Litanies of Satan' presents the unromantic agony of mortals who embrace darkness as if it were heavenly light:

> O Angel, the most brilliant and most wise,
> A God betrayed by fate, deprived of praise,
> Satan, take pity on my misery!
> O prince of exile, you who have been wronged,
> Who, even conquered, rise yet more strong,
> Satan, take pity on my misery!

Satan en route to the modern metropolis: Paul Gavarni, frontispiece to Pierre-Jules Hetzel, pseud. P.-J. Stahl, ed., *Le Diable à Paris* (1845).

> Great king, who know the lore the earth imparts,
> Intimate healer of our anguished hearts,
> Satan, take pity on my misery![60]

Impersonating a priest ministering to a congregation of the 'leprous and despised', Baudelaire calls upon a vanquished ruler who still has tricks up his sleeve. As the 'adoptive father of those ostracized . . . and banished', Satan 'grants the prisoner calm disdain' even when facing execution; he 'sees what whores endure' and gives them strength, and he preserves 'plotters and tramps'.

As per Catholic dogma, humankind is inherently sinful. Still, anyone who would appeal to Satan has a glimmer of spiritual existence; there can be no Devil without God, after all. 'The Murderer's Wine' presents a worst-case scenario: even Satan is repudiated.

> Now I am free and stand alone!
> Dead drunk is what I'll get right here
> And then, without remorse of fear,
> I'll make my bed on dirt and stone
> And sleep as any dog would do!
> That cart with heavy wheels, the truck
> Loaded with rocks and city muck,
> That runaway I welcome to
> Come crush my head, or it might well
> Cut me in half right where I am
> And I don't give a good god-damn
>   [. . . *de Dieu,*]
> For God, Communion, or for Hell!
> [*Du Diable ou de la Sainte Table!*][61]

The killer's self-disgust almost amounts to genuflection: it is only right that one who has shed the blood of another human being wallow in his unclean state. But the last two lines spill over into blasphemy. God may always take mercy on a sinner. Scorn for the Devil, on the other hand, means abandoning even the last illusion of refuge. Nothing is left to save where no hope flickers. Drinking himself into a stupor and hoping for annihilation, the murderer would fuse with inert matter, 'dirt and stone' without a soul to chasten.

The Abject Elite

The 'prince of exile' had travelled far since Milton made him the voice of angels who thought themselves entitled to more than the good Lord would provide. Over time, Satan became a companion in whom poets and artists who were also outcasts – real or imaginary – might confide. Whatever heavenly glory Satan lost, he gained in worldly prestige.

According to predominant ways of thinking in Europe during the eighteenth and nineteenth centuries, human history follows the course of improvement: mounting freedom from superstitious dogma, the extension of civil liberties to more and more people, economic growth, better public services and so on.[62] Yet progress does not benefit everyone all at once. Colonialism, which could be justified as a civilizing mission, is a case in point. What is more, forward strides hardly guarantee that retrograde motion will not occur. When heads of state and captains of industry realized that peoples elsewhere on the globe were not as primitive as their easy conquest suggested, they also discovered 'savages' native to their own lands: the so-called dangerous classes, that is, workers prone to delinquency and political radicals.[63] If time flows, it also eddies and whirls.

With an intuitive grasp of such contradictions, the boy genius Arthur Rimbaud (1854–1891) wrote *A Season in Hell*. This work can be mined for information about his drug- and drink-addled relationship with Paul Verlaine (1844–1896), which ended when the latter fired a pistol at his lover and went to jail. But the point of interest for purposes here is that Rimbaud addresses 'this handful of hideous pages torn from my diary of damnation' to 'dear Satan'.[64]

The highly familiar tone that the author adopts opens onto a space that transcends personal sentiment. Appealing to the Adversary is practically a matter of course for a bohemian *littérateur*. Doing so means cultivating a position among proud pariahs.

> From them I have inherited: idolatry and love of sacrilege; – oh! all the vices, anger, lust . . . above all lying and indolence.
> I abhor every trade. Owners and workers, peasants, the lot of them, mean and petty. The hand which writes is as good as the hand which ploughs. – What a century of hands! – I shall never get my hand in . . . The honesty of begging is too much for me.[65]

Rimbaud stakes out an identity by denying that he belongs to a recognized collective ('I abhor every trade. Owners and workers, peasants, the lot of them . . .'). When he declares that he is sprung from an 'inferior race', he does not have a specific group in mind. Instead, the term signals nameless negativity – an unshaped, inchoate mass as timeless and broad as sin and vice ('idolatry . . . sacrilege . . . anger, lust . . . lying and indolence').

A Season in Hell is a modernist work that rejects modernity.[66] 'Science, the new nobility' garners only scorn: 'Progress. The world strides on! Why might it not also spin?'[67] This bearing seems to conflict with declarations Rimbaud makes elsewhere, notably the so-called *Lettres du voyant*,[68] but he is not contradicting himself so much as rejecting the prevailing view of history. Beyond the Christian civilization that has begotten the cult of science and improvement, the poet reaches back to the time of violent origins and summons forth antediluvian forces. He numbers among 'the children of Ham' reclaiming their birthright.[69]

Rimbaud was 'of the Devil's party', and he knew it. 'I have never been Christian . . . I understand nothing of laws; I have no moral sense, I am an animal.'[70] The poet claims a position of immaturity, exclusion and non-culture to gesture towards raw, untapped energy disclosing new vistas of destructive regeneration.

Fittingly, the last work to have been published in Rimbaud's lifetime is called *Illuminations*. These poems in prose trace fault-lines that would erupt into plain view during the twentieth century. Indeed, they look to the aftermath of the two conflicts in which Europe – or 'Christendom', as it once had been known – squandered the global strength it had amassed by exploiting and subjugating peoples elsewhere. 'As a child, certain skies sharpened the way I saw . . . [Now] I dream of a War, of justice or of might, of logic quite unforeseen.' The *enfant terrible* pictures vengeance as calculated and as cleansing as the terrorist strikes by 'Third World' liberation movements that would occur a few decades later, when, in Frantz Fanon's words, 'the wretched of the earth' expelled their former masters and 'hack[ed] their way into history.'[71]

SIX

Sick, Sick, Sick

Knowledge is power. Unusual intelligence, like exceptional beauty, casts an otherworldly glow. Often it suggests divine guidance or infernal scheming. This explains why the legend of Faust remains so well known. More or less all the 'mad scientists' of nineteenth-century literature are Faust's descendants, from Victor Frankenstein to Drs Jekyll and Moreau. Likewise, the most memorable villains of the twentieth and twenty-first centuries think in dangerous, if not devilish, ways. In *The Silence of the Lambs,* Hannibal Lecter is scary not just because he is a serial killer and a cannibal. He's also a forensic psychiatrist.

During the 1800s natural science proved as vigorous as industrialization, and the fixed order of religious systems yielded more and more to process-oriented conceptions of the world emphasizing metamorphosis and change. Physicians came to hold the position formerly occupied by theologians inasmuch as they possessed privileged insight into the mysteries of mutable existence.[1] The ability to preserve and prolong life implies the potential to destroy it. There is something uncanny about chemistry, biology, medicine and other forms of wonder-working.

On a metaphorical register, 'health' and 'sickness' readily translate into 'good' and 'evil'. But moral fortitude and physiological vigour are not identical. As we will see, a hearty constitution may bespeak spiritual illness, and disease can signify a highly developed sense of right and wrong. This chapter examines literary exercises that play the Devil's advocate to test and try the false certainties and cure-alls of modern optimists. Such 'second opinions' diagnose pathology that afflicts not just individuals but society as a whole.

Poison and Steel

The French novelist Jules-Amédée Barbey d'Aurevilly (1808–1889), who lived and wrote to confound his contemporaries' cheerful prejudice that progress would take care of the fallen human condition, is our first *promotor fidei*.[2] A few years after the author's death, Max Nordau (1849–1923) – also a critic of modernity, but an advocate of rational reform and planning – denounced him as an exemplar of depravity and licentiousness. Barbey, Nordau vituperated, 'stole with utter shamelessness from the books of the Marquis de Sade. That which belongs properly to him is the coloring of Catholic theology he gives to his profligacies.'[3] Nordau championed physical fitness and clean living. He called for a 'muscular' bearing to counter the dissipation and enervation exemplified by France, in particular.[4] As a man of science and an agnostic Jew, he embodied the forward-looking spirit of the nineteenth century; during the long and painful Dreyfus Affair, he became a founding figure of Zionism (which, at the inception, was anything but a religious movement).[5]

Nordau's harsh judgement warrants mention because it represents a way of thinking at odds with everything Barbey prized. For proponents of strength, wholesomeness and vitality, licentious works count as physical threats – agents of infection corrupting the social body. 'Decadence' in literature bespeaks 'degeneration' in culture. Barbey took exception to the hygienic agenda and held to the spiritual nature of art. For him, provocation could trigger intellectual insight and even moral awakening. A dose of wickedness, like a bitter medicine, may produce a salutary effect. Unyielding in his Catholicism, Barbey wrote works with a sulphurous fragrance and a funny taste, elixirs compounded from ingredients more medieval than modern.

'Happiness in Crime' is such a concoction. One of six tales comprising *Diaboliques* (1874), this framed narrative features an enigmatic physician who embodies the ambiguity of the medical trade in the age of positivist science and projects of universal improvement. Doctor Torty sounds like the Devil as Heine had described him a few decades earlier: a man 'of wide research / Who cleverly talks about State and Church'.

> He enjoy[ed] his slightly sacrilegious humor. A genuine disciple of Cabanis in his medical philosophy, he belonged, like his old comrade Chaussier, to that terrifying school of absolute materialism . . .
>
> Doctor Torty was something of a Leatherstocking on horseback . . . A naturalist who scorned social convention . . . Not [having] replaced convention with the idea of a God, he had become one of those pitiless observers who cannot help but become misanthropes.[6]

On the one hand, Torty belongs among scientists who deny the spiritual elements of existence. Pierre Jean Georges Cabanis (1757–1808) wrote *On the Relations Between the Physical and Moral Aspects of Man* (1802); this work would boil the nobler faculties of human intellect and feeling down to nervous processes. His contemporary François Chaussier (1746–1828) was also an unsparing physiologist with little patience for old-fashioned ideas about the human soul.[7] At the same time, Torty has something that makes him alien to the nineteenth century. 'Leatherstocking' is the hero of novels by James Fenimore Cooper, books about the American frontier far, far away from metropolitan Paris. 'Misanthrope' refers to Molière's play of the same name. In this light, Torty occupies a space between historical epochs: the classical age of Louis XIV and the unwritten future of lands overseas.

As the unidentified narrator and his riddling companion stroll through the city, their path leads to an attraction at the Jardin des Plantes. Here, a man and a woman stand watching a caged panther. The pair is just as striking as the beast – and just as out of place. 'A strange thing: with this fine couple, it was the woman who had the muscles, and the man who had the nerves.'[8] She measures nearly the height of her companion, who has a somewhat feminine aspect.[9] Her gaze fastens on the animal with particular intensity. 'Look there – panther versus panther!'[10] Torty whispers, as if lost in a dream.

The stage is set for the real story. Torty, a wily character of 'robust ... and gnarled' stock,[11] belongs to two worlds but adheres to the codes of neither. His name comes from a Latin word meaning 'twisted', 'distorted' or 'tortured', and he delights in paradox and scandal. The not-so-good doctor says that he knows all about the couple's past, which is dark and troubling. 'Finding the beginning . . . is like looking for a bullet after the flesh has closed over the wound,' he hints.[12] As if performing a delicate operation or administering a drug that will prove fatal in excess, Torty proceeds slowly and methodically.

Félicien Rops, 'Happiness in Crime', engraving for J. Barbey d'Aurevilly, *Les Diaboliques* (1886).

This fascinating lady, Torty tells his friend, is the product of a union redolent of impropriety. Her father was an officer 'nicknamed Sabre-tip [*Pointe-au-corps*]' for his skill with the sword.

> After having knocked around all the countries of Europe, and after having had experiences with all the girls that the Devil had put in his path, this old soldier from the first Empire concluded his final love affair by marrying, at the age of fifty, and with all the formalities and sacramental rites, of both the municipality and the Church – a young flirt . . . [She] gave him a child precisely nine months later to the day; and that child, who was a girl, is none other, my friend, than the goddess-like woman we just watched pass.[13]

The father enjoyed social distinction, yet he led a dissolute life. Even his marriage expressed libertinism, for he wed a woman of conspicuously low standing. The birth of the daughter, exactly nine months later, suggests a quickly concluded affair. The nuptials defied polite society in spirit, if not in fact. Torty's reference to 'the Devil' may or may not be a figure of speech.

The striking woman in the Jardin des Plantes is a civilized monster. She owes her divine appearance to the appetites of a man who delighted in war and amorous conquest. Torty pointedly observes that her godfather, 'a knight of the order of Saint Louis and a captain of dragoons before the Revolution', was cut from the same cloth. An 'inveterate talker' given to 'tossing off sarcastic remarks right along with his ferocious swordplay', it was he who named her.[14] 'Hauteclaire' is synonymous with a deadly weapon: 'the daughter of a man like you,' the godfather told Sabre-tip, 'should have a name like that of a valiant knight's sword.'[15]

'Despite the liberals and their constant whining, there was and always will be an indestructible bond between the nobility and the clergy,' Torty says in a sly aside:

The priest . . . grimaced a bit at this name that had never been heard at the baptismal font of his church, but . . . since, as it happens, there is a saint named Claire in the Roman calendar, the name of [the] épée was . . . given to the child.[16]

No further mention of the mother is made. Hauteclaire sprang from a confidence and intimacy between men that bordered on perversity, and she was christened when her bullying father twisted the arm of a priest who hesitated but complied. A veneer of Christian decorum covers the fruit of sinful dalliances, a pagan lust for life.

In adolescence the girl followed in the footsteps of her father and godfather. When Sabre-tip died, Mademoiselle Hauteclaire Stassin took over the fencing academy that her sire had founded. In parting from a conventional feminine role, 'this young girl who had no wealth or resource apart from her sword' won the hearts of 'the richest young men in town.'[17] She refused all other admirers for a suitor who belonged to another woman. Taking the position of a domestic servant, she conspired with her beloved to poison his wife so she might fulfill her own 'destiny'.[18] Ever since, in keeping with the biblical phrase, the two have been 'one flesh' (Genesis 2:24, Mark 10:8, Ephesians 5:31).

No judgement is passed in the story itself or in the frame narrative; the events cannot be verified, anyway. Torty might just be spinning a yarn, or his every word could be true. In either case the tale of the terrible woman and the refined but dissolute lineage to which she belongs offers a picture that contradicts the values of the modern world on every score. For Hauteclaire and her kind, rank and right pass through the blood, and arcane ritual consecrates them. A free society of equals united in republican brotherhood (or sisterhood) exists only as an obstacle – or a hunting ground. That is why, on a primordial level, Hauteclaire is a 'panther': no matter how much the world may seem to have changed over years, decades, centuries and millennia, the law of the jungle still holds. And the law of the jungle is the law of the strong and cunning.

Barbey's devilish work is arranged to pose a test. The first-person narrator is simply going about his everyday business when he strikes upon Torty, a man of his acquaintance whom he doesn't know *that* well. Should he trust the doctor? On the one hand, Torty is a vivid and engaging storyteller – perfect company. On the other, if what he says is true, it must derive from personal involvement in wicked deeds. Should Torty be an accomplice to murder, or even 'just' an accessory after the fact, social intercourse with him ought to be avoided. Torty is a foreign body and a possible agent of contamination. Through this ambiguous figure with a silver tongue who 'go[es] to and fro in the earth', Barbey practises in literature what his contemporary Louis Pasteur (1822–1895) pioneered in medicine: vaccination and immunology, but with moral antibodies.

Everything wants to live and prosper – and often at the expense of other living things. The lesson of 'Happiness in Crime' is that one should not think the beauties of the world are there just to be contemplated and enjoyed, nor should one think that cosmic forces are not at work at all places and at all times. In the shadows of the splendours we behold, a universe of good and evil exists, too. Through Torty, Barbey administers a tiny dram of poison to strengthen our constitution in an age that too readily mistakes bodily health for spiritual weal. Who has not pursued personal advantage to the detriment of others? Hauteclaire represents an extreme example, but her animal instincts are perfectly natural.

'Happiness in Crime' may be a fabrication through and through, but the pleasures of diversion, literary or otherwise, are not innocent. What critics used to call 'suspension of disbelief' actually means crediting what, one can only hope, is falsehood. Torty's narrative brings out the real complicity of imaginary engagement. In every scene that unfolds, he is somehow there – not centre stage, but present. When the story of 'this fine couple' is over, he comes to the fore again, winking and grinning like the very Devil. Ideally, the 'gentle reader' will feel a little unwell.

Spiritual and Social Disease

Torty, who supposedly belongs to 'that terrifying school of absolute materialism' which dissects the soul and finds only a haywire of nerves, is actually an unreconstructed metaphysician. The story he tells points both to the cruelty and selfishness of the human animal and to a provision in the unknowable plans of the Lord that allows for vice to go unpunished – at least for the moment. The diabolical doctor pops up in the modern metropolis to trouble an idle conscience on 'one of those sunny, clear autumn days that keep the swallows from departing.'[19]

'Happiness in Crime' harbours obscurity that invites doubt and interpretation. Creation holds marvels and terrors, and each beat of the human heart affirms life even as it moves one step closer to the final hour – and the Last Judgement. In the meanwhile, Satan 'deceiveth the whole world' (Revelation 12:9).

The ominous calm evoked by Barbey, the arch-Catholic, contrasts with the picture presented by his secular contemporary Karl Marx, who had no patience for reactionary dandies or theological sophistry.[20] In a host of polemical articles and studies, the political economist exposed the workings of relations of production that obstruct fulfilment for hardworking men and women in the world here and now.

Marx was descended from rabbis on both sides. He rejected both his ancestors' faith and his father's Lutheranism by charting his own course in the wake of Georg Wilhelm Friedrich Hegel (1770–1831) and Ludwig Feuerbach (1804–1879). Hegel gave Marx a philosophy of history that he used to portray class struggle as the motor of social and cultural evolution from antiquity to the present day. Feuerbach taught him that humankind fashions its own gods. Religion expresses an inner striving; the God of Judeo-Christian civilization, like the pagan deities of old, represents human potential, not an external power. In lieu of merely 'interpreting the world', Marx called on his fellow human beings 'to change it'.[21] Although he would surely have denied as much, he thereby renewed the militancy of the ancient prophets.

Capitalism, according to Marx, sustains itself by generating illusions that conceal real conditions of exploitation. He calls the mendacious wonders of this religion without a soul 'commodity fetishism'. Workers give their sweat and blood, but the fruits of labour go on to be sold for the profit of others, who produce nothing at all. Material expenditure turns into an item of exchange, which undergoes another transformation when viewed in terms of money. Money is 'something' that is not really a thing because, even when given the form of a coin or a note, its substance is immaterial. As if by black magic, it confers the vitality extracted from real human beings onto objects that now seem to lead lives of their own. Commodities amount to the 'idols [of] wood and stone' (Deuteronomy 29:17) denounced in the Bible, dead images radiating false vitality. Industrialists, bankers and anyone else who performs no physical labour but derives benefit from it are the temple bureaucracy of modern-day Egypt, as it were. For want of insight into this process of mystification, people who might yet reach the Promised Land of a classless society lose their inborn grandeur and come to serve 'strange gods' (Joshua 24:23).

Marx steps forward as an accuser to advocate on behalf of the 'despised', the 'ostracized' and the 'banished'.[22] A more equitable order is possible. Guided by their better angels, people can recognize – and then change – conditions that keep individuals, societies and the species as a whole from living in harmony; the world's riches are enough to provide for all. Once unjust relations have been laid bare, human beings working together in good faith will be able to set them right. Religion casts a long shadow.

On another level, which Marx and his adherents would be more inclined to acknowledge, the operative paradigm is medical science. The cause for alienation and pathology lies in the disequilibrium of life in community. Observe the proper regime and the organism will heal. The balanced flow of resources corresponds to healthy blood flow, a sturdy digestive system and so on. The imbalance between microcosm and macrocosm can be righted by 'scientific socialism'.[23] Modern innovations for the better will correct modern developments for the worse.

In younger years, Barbey's friend Léon Bloy (1846–1917) was inclined to agree with diagnoses offered by the freethinkers and atheists in the milieu to which Marx and fellow travellers belonged.[24] Indeed, he did so in maturity, but now he drew different conclusions. Instead of turning to the future for improvement, he looked to the mythical past for confirmation that mortal endeavours are doomed. Humankind has always been unwell. This is what the story of Eden means: as soon as Adam and Eve ate from the Tree of Knowledge, they left the paradise of nature, where they had lived as simply and straightforwardly as beasts. Ever since, their descendants have inhabited the gulf of sin their first parents opened.

Bloy's *Exegesis of the Commonplaces* (1902; published in an expanded version some ten years later) is conceived along lines similar to those of *The Devil's Dictionary* (1906/11) by the American writer Ambrose Bierce, which appeared around the same time half a world away. But if Bierce was an unbeliever and a cynic whose writings dismantled religious bigotry and prejudice, Bloy used his diabolical wit to affirm a Catholicism so rigorous the legendary Inquisition might have recoiled in horror.[25] *Exegesis of the Commonplaces* treats proverbial expressions and everyday turns of phrase as pearls of wisdom that have become so encrusted with filth in passing from one set of unclean hands to the next that they appear utterly worthless.

Bloy sets out to polish the ancient currency and show what commonplaces mean from the standpoint of eternity – the sole standard that really holds for Christians, whether they like it or not. *Exegesis of the Commonplaces* seems to be written in the voice of the biblical accuser – Satan himself – making trial of the unrighteous against the backdrop of universal decadence. To take one example among many others, Bloy glosses the phrase 'To be in business' as follows:

That means, for the bourgeois, being seated on great thrones of gold to judge the world. His is an aristocracy next to which all other aristocracies are a little less than shit. Peers and grandees would consider themselves lucky to serve most humbly, if only things were as they should be. As for artists and abject wretches who still employ their capacity to think: what base tasks should they be assigned?[26]

The bourgeois views everything in venal terms. This bearing levels all differences: 'No matter what, it gets sold. It can be cheese, wine, horses, jewelry, garden tools, bridal wreaths, rendered carcasses, or whatever happens to get scraped up – it just has to sell.' Commerce makes the ineffable qualities of objects disappear; 'cheese' and 'wine' become interchangeable with 'rendered carcasses' for capitalist vulgarians on the make. On a subjective register, human relations grow denatured, too: 'Lying, stealing, poisoning, pimping and whoring, betrayal, sacrilege, and apostasy are honorable when you're in business.' Buying and selling for profit bespeaks bankruptcy, no matter how rich one gets, for it lacks a spiritual dimension. Those who place stock in the world of trade have no use for what is useless and, by the same token, sublime: art, thinking or any other pursuit that defies financial calculation.

Theological insight means awareness of inadequacy, especially one's own. Human intelligence seeks – and finds – remedies to many ills, but it cannot fix the one problem underlying all others: being 'as gods' (Genesis 3:5) without, in fact, *being* gods. Knowledge of good and evil does not amount to the ability, much less the will, to act. And even when action is possible, mortal judgement remains prone to error and perverseness. Bloy deadpans: 'Understand what I'm saying . . . The seller is always . . . a miracle worker with the power to give to God the Father what belongs to the Holy Ghost . . . [It's] really quite simple. Money . . . is the Redeemer.' Modern society follows the liturgy of the market. Those who manage to scramble to the top of the dogpile of fraudulent miracle workers replace belief with credit, guilt with debt and religion with superstition. The deals the bourgeois sniff out stink to high heaven.

Much of *Exegesis of the Commonplaces* could be mistaken for a Marxist jeremiad. Today, 'bourgeoisie' and related terms are associated with left-wing polemics. In the long nineteenth century, however, reactionaries who wished to preserve Church and Crown agreed with social radicals advocating a world free of inherited rank. Both right and left faulted the socio-economic centre for being exactly what it was: mediocre, especially in a moral sense. For parties on one end of the political spectrum, the bourgeois incarnated the vices of the social climber without distinction or refinement. For those on the other end, this type was content to rest in smug self-satisfaction after securing his own self-interest; the bourgeois could be roused to action only to combat unfortunates beneath him trying to better their lot, too. The aristocracy and the proletariat had values pegged to the past and the future, respectively. The bourgeois stood for nothing, yet his kind commanded the present.

Bloy may have switched allegiances from Voltairean provocation to hardline Catholicism, but he remained committed to absolutes. Although hardly a saint, he made a virtue of his failings, embracing poverty and suffering as the keys to heaven. This position of voluntary abasement authorized him to rail like a prophet against a world as corrupt as anything ever witnessed in ancient times, when people – however sinful and stupid they might have been – still knew the fear of God. Those who prosper in a corrupt society deserve a thrashing like the one Jesus famously gave 'them that sold and bought in the temple' (Matthew 21:12).

However much Bloy's sermons from the depths shock conventional sensibilities, they cut with the precision of a surgeon's instrument and leave as little room for objection as a medieval syllogism. The Bible is an open book, available to all. If the finer points of its teachings elude the multitude, then the fault lies with them. That said, understanding the basic code should not prove terribly difficult. The triumphs and travails of the ancient Jews are plain: when they acted in keeping with divine will, they bested the worst of enemies; when they failed to do so, they were punished. The New Testament adopts a gentler tone. God's covenant extends to all who welcome the Saviour. Yet if joining the elect is a blessing, it also imposes harsh demands. There is no way to achieve salvation if one disregards Christ's plain-spoken injunctions to love one's brethren and act charitably. The pursuit of 'filthy lucre' – to say nothing of other forms of misconduct – is prohibited. How many of those who profess the faith abide by God's commandments?

Nominal Christians fondling charmed baubles (money) and fawning before statues (commodities) like savages have earned the 'wages of sin': death (Romans 6:23). Like a leprous apostle, Bloy reveled in breaking the rules of polite society to promulgate the Law of the Kingdom. 'Humble yourselves . . . under the mighty hand of God, that he may exalt you in due time . . . Be sober, be vigilant, because your adversary the Devil, as a roaring lion, walketh about, seeking whom he may devour' (1 Peter 5:6–8).

The Soul of a Monster

Life on earth is so confusing that some missteps surely warrant pardon; symbols and flags can point in the opposite direction of what they mean. 'Satan himself is transformed into an angel of light,' one reads in the Pauline epistles (2 Corinthians 11:14). From the nineteenth century on, socialists and communists have crusaded for ideals that sound, for all the world, like those of the Christian Gospel. And since ancient times, there have been religious leaders who called for the destruction of the standing order in the name of the Lord. Marx might at points be mistaken for a full-blooded zealot (a word that originally referred to a Jewish sect uncompromisingly opposed to Rome and polytheism[27]). Conversely, Bloy professed a faith so absolute its mystical bent bordered on nihilism.

At the end of *The Last Columns of the Church* (1903), Bloy launches a polemic against those who have made bold to declare themselves Catholic when their every word fumes like incense on a pagan altar.

> Lord Jesus! I would prefer you have no house at all. Look at these columns, which block your very sight, even from afar . . . Give me the strength of Samson to cast down to the ground, once and for all, this den of thieves and imbeciles more remorseless than murderers.[28]

The targets of Bloy's invective include the novelist Joris-Karl Huysmans (1848–1907), guilty of retreating into delicate aestheticism when religion demands alms for the poor and washing the feet of beggars. Huysmans may not have deserved such opprobrium. Only a man 'fanatically ungrateful' – as Bloy said of himself – could fault an erstwhile friend for not going far enough in writing a novel that denounces 'the diabolical curia' of 'tonsured magicians' populating the Vatican.[29] Huysmans was also appalled by the world he lived in. Unlike his rabid contemporary, he exhibited the restraint befitting a civil servant – the quiet profession he exercised.

Huysmans' *Là-Bas* (1891) tells the story of a writer working on a book about Gilles de Rais, the fifteenth-century nobleman who defiled, tortured and killed hundreds of children.[30] Durtal – a thinly concealed version of Huysmans himself – surmises that 'Satanism has come down in a straight, unbroken line' from medieval times to his own day.[31] In the course of his studies, he comes to recognize that he is somewhat mistaken: modern Satanists fall short of their wicked forebear.

Little happens in *Là-Bas*. For the most part, the novel records the protagonist's conversations with his friend Des Hermies, a blasé doctor who despises his profession because it offers no remedy for the malady from which all men and women are suffering. In this morbidly sensitive age, he observes, people's 'nerves quiver at the least shock', and medicine does not afford the slightest help.[32] Like Durtal, Des Hermies finds his contemporaries disenchanted, dull and irritating. He would probably say the same of his companion and himself, if the great unwashed did not provide such an easy target for abuse. The two malcontents compete in uncharitable assessments of their fellow human beings running about under the spell of slogans and empty phrases.

Oozing melancholy and spleen, the man of letters and the man of science would like nothing so much as to escape the modern world. Gazing into the void that surrounds them, they rhapsodize about another time. A wholly different spirit animated the medieval universe:

> No doubt . . . [it] was a singular epoch . . . For some it's all white, and for others utterly black. No intermediate shade, the history professors and atheists reiterate. Dolorous and exquisite epoch, say the artists and the religious savants.[33]

In contrast to the whirl and tumble of the nineteenth century, there used to be 'immutable classes'. When people still respected the cosmic order incarnated by clergy and nobility, they 'had loftier souls'. Now, opinions and mores come and go in dissolute tides. 'Society has done nothing but deteriorate in the four centuries separating us from the Middle Ages.'[34]

Avoiding other company, Durtal and Des Hermies often pay visit to a poor but virtuous couple for dinner. Despite his modest station as a bell-ringer, Carhaix possesses sapience as precious as a holy relic.[35] Des Hermies describes the man's devotion to the vanished age:

> Carhaix would be broken-hearted if he lost his bells . . . The bell is an instrument in a class of its own. It is baptized like a Christian, anointed with sacramental oil, and according to the pontifical rubric it is also to be sanctified, by a bishop, in seven cruciform unctions . . .
>
> It is . . . the herald of the Church, the voice from without as the priest is the voice from within.[36]

Up in an 'aerial tomb',[37] by the bells Carhaix reveres, the two misanthropes find refuge from the universal idiocy 'down there' (*là-bas*). The juxtaposition corresponds to the difference between then and now. Here, a glimmer of immortal futurity appears in the remnants of past piety.

The culminating event of the novel occurs against the backdrop of hope all but eclipsed by *ennui*: Durtal's attendance of a modern-day black mass. Now, as always, the Adversary stands for testing and trial. Empiricism and fieldwork will provide data to support or refute the writer's thesis that Satanism still thrives. The experiment proves bitterly disappointing. If the world today has abandoned God, it has betrayed the Devil, too.

Durtal gains access to the underground sphere of so-called Satanists through the mediation of one Madame Chantelouve. This woman, whose name means 'song of the she-wolf', is the wife of a pitiful man who fawns upon the lions of the publishing world to sell his hack writing about the lives of the saints. Madame Chantelouve has initiated correspondence with Durtal because she sees a reflection of her own alienated existence in his gloomy books. Surely, they are kindred spirits. Durtal is agnostic about how much they really share, but he agrees to a tryst: Madame Chantelouve has told him she knows a practitioner of the dark arts. The man he is studying, Gilles de Rais, is supposed to have made a pact with the Devil. What better way to connect with his subject than by witnessing the knight's modern-day counterpart?

Alas, like everything else in the corrupted nineteenth century, the experience might not be worth the effort. Obscurity does not necessarily signify depth. The liaison with the adulteress leaves Durtal more disgusted than ever with himself, with her and with humanity in general. Pollution of the flesh with Madame Chantelouve raises the curtain for a spectacle of metaphysical horror at the black mass itself.

The throng that gathers for the service presents a piteous sight: riff-raff washed off the streets without a hold even in the gutter. These desperate souls' last hope is that Satan – whom they invoke as a 'reasonable God', a 'just God' – will reverse their misfortune. A defrocked priest performs the ceremony:

> Suzerain of Resentment, Accountant of Humiliations, Treasurer of old Hatreds, thou alone dost fertilize the brain of man whom injustice has crushed; thou breathest into him the idea of meditated vengeance, sure misdeeds; thou incitest him to murder; thou givest him the abundant joy of accomplished reprisals and permittest him to taste the intoxicating draught of the tears of which he is the cause.[38]

The oration appeals to 'Resentment . . . Humiliations [and] Hatreds'. In other words, the officiant accepts indignity and revels in it. Enjoining others to do the same, he would make what is already bad even worse. Any 'man whom injustice has crushed' should go forth to seek 'vengeance' and 'murder'. Bloody 'reprisals' promise 'abundant joy', a taste of the 'intoxicating draught of . . . tears'. Calling for their affliction to be remedied in this world instead of the next plunges the congregants even deeper into the filth and viciousness that have already soaked them to the bone. Redressing a wrong does not guarantee that the right thing will be done, and so too suffering need not beget virtue.

The message propagated at the ceremony runs counter to the Christian doctrine of forgiveness. Nothing like justice can occur by suspending the rule of law and declaring a murderous free-for-all. But what offends Durtal – and the author who has written himself into the character – is not immorality so much as bad taste, the herd mentality of the congregation.

Yielding to emotion and impulse means turning away from past and future alike. Only the convulsive present remains: automatism mistaken for willed action.

> The women fell to the carpet and writhed. One of them seemed to be worked by a spring. She threw herself prone and waved her legs in the air. Another . . . clucked, then . . . stood with her mouth open . . . Another, inflated, livid, her pupils dilated, lolled her head back over her shoulders, then jerked it brusquely erect and belaboured herself, tearing her breast with her nails. Another, sprawling on her back, undid her skirts . . .[39]

Mass hysteria erupts. The worshippers take revenge for life's disappointments and their foiled desires by indulging in sexual carnage that leaves only a pile of spent bodies. The scene represents everything that already ails the world, taken *ad absurdum* and *ad nauseam*.

The novel's rub lies in the sublimity Huysmans's alter ego sees in the story of a real Satanist, which provides a foil to the antics of the 'modern Gilles de Rais' and his hangers-on.[40] In the Middle Ages 'the elect of Evil' had to make a supreme effort to 'descend to the last step of the spiral'.[41] The historical Gilles de Rais did not pretend that divine law might be disregarded with impunity, much less updated or replaced. Nor did he violate the Commandments out of resentment. Having lucidly embraced evil, he towers above modern-day lowlifes ignorant of the grandeur of Sin.

Indignities that Satan faces in the modern world: Adolphe Block, *Satan Journaliste*, 1860s, hand-coloured albumen silver print.

Durtal all but flies, in his mind's eye, to a sabbath of his own. The ruthless nobleman, he surmises, was on a quest to leave the material world behind by means of the outrages he perpetrated. As a corrective to the spiritual beggary of his own day, when neither the Lord nor the Devil receives due respect, Durtal envisions monstrous scenes in the past. In this picture, Gilles de Rais arranges for accomplices to torture children to the point of death; then, he rushes in and offers comfort – before killing them more gruesomely still. 'His ferocity [did] not remain merely carnal . . . He wishe[d] to make [victims] suffer both in body and soul.'[42] Like the Marquis de Sade's libertines, he exhausts himself trying to multiply transgression to infinite dimensions; unlike Sade's butchers, he performs acts of sacrifice to attain the Absolute, the agony of Abraham with his knife at his son's throat or the desolation of the disciples who abandon Jesus in his final hours.

And so, Durtal/Huysmans deploys a circuitous logic worthy of the most cunning Jesuit to affirm the one true Church; Gilles is the paragon of the fallen human condition, perversely trying to pluck fruit from 'the tree of knowledge of good and evil' (Genesis 2:9). In the tapestry the novelist weaves, the Adversary is vindicated. 'If in Love . . . the infinite is approachable for certain souls, the . . . possibilities of Evil are limited.' 'Human imagination' has boundaries, and Satan 'dupes all persons who give themselves . . . to him.'[43]

The Devil retains his testing role and ultimately serves to promote Good. Even as Gilles heaps crime upon crime, nothing will satisfy him. His own life is ceaseless agony on a rack of his own contrivance:

As he can descend no further, he tries returning on the way by which he has come, but now remorse overtakes him, overwhelms him, and wrenches him without respite. His nights are nights of expiation. Besieged by phantoms, he howls like a wounded beast. He is found rushing along the solitary corridors of the château. He weeps, throws himself on his knees, swears to God that he will do penance. He promises to found pious institutions . . . He speaks of shutting himself up in a cloister, of going to Jerusalem, begging his bread on the way.[44]

Nineteenth-century minds simply cannot fathom such depths – or heights. When wickedness finally exhausts him, the butcher repents sincerely. Gilles faces certain doom on earth, but the Eternal Judge may yet pardon him.

Nothing of the sort is even thinkable in the godless and hypocritical modern world. Where's Satan when you need him?

How to Philosophize with a Scalpel

Barbey, Bloy and Huysmans wielded the pen like a knife to wound self-contented sensibilities. They earned the title of 'decadent' because critics and readers took them at their word.[45] Such a reputation is not wholly unmerited, but these writers thought they were examining the morbid state of European civilization, which they certainly had not created. The substance of 'style' is *cutting* (from Latin *stilus*, 'pointed instrument'). Decadent exercises in style are operations to remove bad blood. A deft stroke can heal.

Our diabolical authors also practised the physician's art inasmuch as the right measure of a pathogen may prove beneficial. None of them would have put matters in such terms, but their view of evil agreed with scientific germ theory. Recognizing just how easily disease spreads, they wrote to inoculate their contemporaries with the potent dogma of Original Sin. In their eyes, the most pernicious myth of modern times is Jean-Jacques Rousseau's idea that 'man' started out virtuous – hale, hearty and free – only to become denatured and depraved by foreign contaminants.[46]

Significantly, the craftiest surgeon of the day did not spring from irredentist Catholic stock. Antiseptic German Protestantism brought forth Friedrich Nietzsche (1844–1900), the exemplary diagnostician – and would-be destroyer – of the sickness afflicting the world.[47] A master of paradox and provocation, Nietzsche is famous for the incendiary statement 'God is dead.' The declaration has made his name synonymous with blasphemy in the popular mind. But these words (and similarly outrageous pronouncements) need to be read in context.

Without attention to irony and style, one fails to grasp the philosopher's point:

> God is dead. God remains dead. And we have killed him. How shall we comfort ourselves, the murderers of all murderers? What was holiest and mightiest of all that the world has yet owned has bled to death under our knives: who will wipe this blood off us? What water is there for us to clean ourselves? What festivals of atonement, what sacred games shall we have to invent? Is not the greatness of this deed too great for us? Must we ourselves not become gods simply to appear worthy of it?[48]

Nietzsche entitled this passage 'The Madman'. The title identifies the speaker as insane. Those who are called mad do not interact with others in a way that admits mutual understanding; their perspective counts as warped, defective or illogical. Yet the incomprehensibility of 'mad' discourse does not necessarily stem from an internal flaw. Communication may fail because listeners are inattentive, prejudiced or simply stupid. When words fly in the face of convention and common understanding, the individual voicing them gets written off as a lunatic; sometimes people aren't ready. Prophets are rarely heeded by their contemporaries.

To appreciate Nietzsche's dictum, one must entertain the possibility that the real madness lies with us. 'God is dead' is hardly a declaration to be understood in terms of ordinary logic or grammar. God commands both life and death. He can do anything at any time – including rise from the dead. In fact Nietzsche's madman is indicting those who would rather not face up to their own actions. The problem lies with human beings who have made bold to contend against the Lord. 'Is not the greatness of this deed too great for us?' Nietzsche is saying the very opposite of what uncritical readers have taken him to mean. People may neglect and dishonour God, but they cannot kill Him. The very idea is crazy.

The larger thrust of Nietzsche's argument concerns human presumption – specifically, the hubris of modern European civilization. 'We' are 'the murderers of all murderers', the sickest and most violent creatures ever to have existed, inasmuch as we think that our accomplishments have elevated us above the station of our ancestors in ancient times or 'primitives' elsewhere on the globe.[49] We would need to 'become gods' to 'wipe this blood off' – a Promethean endeavour of sanitation.

Seeming improvement masks an eternally recurring drive for dominance. Nietzsche's misunderstood doctrine of the 'will to power' simply means that overt, physical force has a metaphysical correlate: from acts of charity to pronouncements of universal law, everything that human beings do serves the ulterior purpose of attaining divine status, which is impossible.

Ernst Bertram, one of Nietzsche's most influential early commentators, aptly remarked that the philosopher offered the 'strongest thesis of an *advocatus diaboli*' to date.

[For] Nietzsche . . . evil is of divine origin, indeed a highest characteristic of everything that he calls divine . . . In a playfully malicious manner, but certainly not in an unserious one, [he] makes God the father of evil: 'Speaking theologically . . . it was God himself who at the end of his day's work laid himself under the tree as a snake: thus he rested from being God.'[50]

In other words, the philosopher notorious for styling himself as an 'immoralist' recognized that it makes no sense to apply the categories of good and evil to the Author of the World.[51] His 'playfully malicious manner' shows the frankness and irony that a lawyer, when making a case, is allowed to display in court.

The Eternal Judge will decide as He sees fit. God can do, and be, whatever He wishes. He is not, and never has been, on trial. Why shouldn't He have a sense of humour? No mortal may prescribe anything to the Lord. If Nietzsche ultimately went mad, he, the Devil's advocate, might have been in on the joke.

SEVEN

The Godawful Truth

Without a higher dimension to existence, the human animal stands, falls, crawls and perishes as a beast among beasts. The cruel wit of Joseph de Maistre (1753–1821), an untiring defender of Church and Crown, makes as much plain. His *St Petersburg Dialogues* (1821) insists on the divine order of Creation by way of a limit-case: war. 'The functions of the soldier are terrible', one of the interlocutors observes, 'but they must result from a great law of the spiritual world'. After all, 'every nation . . . is united in seeing in this scourge something still more peculiarly divine than in others.'[1]

When performing his duty, the soldier does not belong to himself: transcending self-interest, he is sanctified because he acts to fulfil a superior will. Neither eros nor death is what it seems from a higher standpoint. 'The true warrior, amid the blood he sheds, is humane, just as the wife is chaste in the transports of love.'[2]

On this basis, Maistre's *porte-parole* demonstrates the law governing the earth:

In the immense sphere of living things, the obvious rule is violence, a kind of inevitable frenzy which arms all things *in mutua funera.* Once you leave the world of insensible substances, you find the decree of violent death written on the very frontiers of life. Even in the vegetable kingdom, this law can be perceived ... But once you enter the animal kingdom, the law suddenly becomes frighteningly obvious. A power at once hidden and palpable appears constantly occupied in bringing to light the principle of life by violent means. In each great division of the animal world, it has chosen a certain number of animals charged with devouring the others ... There is not an instant of time when some living creature is not devoured by another. Above all these numerous animal species is placed man, whose destructive hand spares no living thing.[3]

Carnage and chaos are everywhere, but the watchful eye discerns a hidden pattern. Subtle gradations of power mean that the general law of mutual antagonism does not occur on a level plane; instead, asymmetries extend to a single point in the heavens. 'An occult ... law demanding human blood' leads to the summit, where God has His throne.[4]

This chapter stands apart from the rest of the study in that it largely omits discussion of the Adversary in order to focus on visions of the Almighty. If Satan is not there to chasten and correct, mortals must face their Maker directly. In the late nineteenth and early twentieth centuries, when self-willed authors and intellectuals sought to break with practices and beliefs now deemed obsolete, they rediscovered the ancient verity Maistre had affirmed a few decades earlier: 'The Lord most high is terrible' (Psalm 47:2). Satan is just a tester. God commands life and death.

Heretical Ardour

Historian Peter Gay has argued that 'the lure of heresy' accounts for the phenomenon of modernism, which stretched from the middle of the nineteenth century to the middle of the twentieth. The 'sheer act of . . . insubordination against ruling authority' unites a vast array of poets, composers, artists and intellectuals more notable for their differences than for shared qualities or a common milieu.[5] Gay begins with Baudelaire, who, as we have seen, gave free rein to blasphemy to profess his adherence to the Church's teachings. This exemplary modernist appreciated the libertarian socialism of Pierre-Joseph Proudhon (1809–1865) but also admired Maistre,[6] tending 'flowers of evil' that offended profane sensibilities; the shocked incomprehension of clerics and censors electrified him as much as the crush of insurrectionary mobs or divine judgement crashing down like lightning.

James Joyce (1882–1941) is another textbook illustration of the modernist heretic. *Ulysses* (1922) combines shifting narrative perspectives, stream-of-consciousness discourse, encyclopaedic erudition and scatological humour. Tellingly, both of the novel's protagonists confront nagging questions of religious and cultural inheritance. The atheistic Stephen Dedalus is haunted by his refusal to pray over his mother as she lay dying, and he ambivalently harbours the dream of becoming a national poet of Ireland, the land he loves and loathes. Leopold Bloom is Jewish enough to be mocked for his ancestry on his father's side, even though he is uncircumcised and has received Christian baptism.

Joyce belonged to Baudelaire's tribe, if for no other reason than the fact that he worked with inherited forms to build a monument to his own perverse power of invention. Ancient mysteries abide in the twentieth century: 'Jewgreek is greekjew. Extremes meet. Death is the highest form of life. Bah!'[7]

As Gay observes, modernism was 'compatible with virtually every creed, including conservatism ... and with virtually every dogma from atheism to Catholicism'.[8] Insubordination does not always seek to abolish authority, and aesthetic radicalism can represent a complement or an alternative to political action. Heresy, which means 'self-chosen opinion', is no metaphor in this context.[9]

Modernism takes flight beyond appointed limits. First and final things are inexorable – and so is God. 'Real' or not, the Deity signifies the sum total of the institutions, ideologies and laws governing human existence.

A lesser-known case is *Les chants de Maldoror*. Little is known about the author, Isidore Ducasse (1846–1870), who adopted the pseudonym 'Comte de Lautréamont' for print and died at a very young age. Posthumously, he achieved celebrity among avant-garde artists – especially the Surrealists, who devised a veritable hagiography of their forebear for want of biographical information.[10]

Whoever the author really was, he was a heretic's heretic. His vision of God is not easy to forget.

One day ... tired of trudging along the steep track of earthly voyage and of staggering like a drunkard through life's dark catacombs, I ... dared penetrate the mysteries of heaven! ... I raised my dismayed gaze ... until I caught sight of a throne fashioned of human excrement and gold upon which, with idiotic pride, body swathed in a shroud made of unwashed hospital sheets, sat he who calls himself the Creator! He held

Spiritualism without spirituality: Odilon Redon, *Dream*, 1878–82, etching on paper.

in his hand a corpse's decaying torso and bore it in turn from eyes to nose, from nose to mouth . . . His feet were immersed in a vast pool of blood, to whose surface two or three cautious heads would suddenly rise like tapeworms from a full chamberpot, and immediately slip back again quick as arrows: a well-applied kick on the bridge of the nose was the familiar reward for breach of rules . . .

Amphibians at best, they swam between two waters in that loathsome liquid!

And then the Creator . . . would with the first two claws of his foot seize [a] swimmer by the neck as in a vice, and raise him from the reddish slime . . . into the air . . . First of all he would devour head, legs, and arms, and lastly the trunk, until nothing was left.[11]

Fuller sacrilege is hard to picture. 'He who calls himself the Creator' looks like a monstrous child, seated 'with idiotic pride' on 'excrement' and destroying its toys. His 'beard clotted' with the 'brains' of unfortunates who provide a horrible repast, God equally resembles a senile lunatic compensating for lost potency by annihilating the spawn once sprung from his loins. 'Sometimes he would exclaim: "I have created you, so I have the right to do with you what I will. You have done nothing against me, that I do not deny. And for my pleasure, I make you suffer."'[12] Like a latter-day John of Patmos, 'Lautréamont' reveals an awful secret: medieval depictions of Hell showed Heaven, and images of Satan devouring sinners portrayed the true face of the Lord. The tester represents just one part of the divine order, and he is not even necessary. Whatever ills mortals encounter begin and end with God, whether He is fit to judge or not.

Feverish and hallucinatory scenes drip with vital energy on every page. It is not difficult to understand the work's appeal to artists intent on bringing the world of dreams into waking life and scandalizing conventional sensibilities. *Les chants de Maldoror* reads like a lucid nightmare. That said, there is no telling what intentions the author had. Technically, 'Lautréamont' is part of the fiction, a made-up persona identical with the title figure, Maldoror. The book wantonly shifts from first- to third-person narration and back again. Should the reader lack 'rigorous logic and mental application at least tough enough to balance his distrust, the deadly issues of this book will lap up his soul as water does sugar'.[13]

Les chants de Maldoror might all be a monstrous joke.[14] Even so, it represents a sovereign act of imagination and style. Baudelaire would have appreciated the feints and dodges of his 'hypocritical brother', had he lived long enough to read them. An essay from his venomous quill, 'On the Essence of Laughter', identifies the nexus between mirth and despair. 'Since laughter is essentially human it is essentially contradictory', Baudelaire notes,

> that is to say it is at one and the same time a sign of infinite greatness and of infinite wretchedness, infinite wretchedness in relation to the absolute being, of whom man has an inkling, infinite greatness in relation to the beasts. It is from the constant clash of these two infinites that laughter flows.[15]

It's funny: modernist heretics might bend the rules and even cheat, but the game started long ago. Sometimes they play a winning hand, but the cards are stacked and the house is dealing. The bluff cannot go on forever.

The high modern hilarity offered by the German author Oskar Panizza (1853–1921) testifies to 'infinite wretchedness and infinite greatness'. In the words of his incredulous contemporary, the novelist Theodor Fontane (1819–1898), 'They ought to erect either a stake for him or a monument. Our public should finally learn that atheism also has its heroes and martyrs.'[16] Panizza's most well-known work is *The Love Council* (1894). This play, about the outbreak of syphilis in Europe, stages life at the dissolute court of Pope Alexander VI – Rodrigo Borgia – with equally scandalous scenes in Heaven and Hell: God is a doddering old man, Christ a weak-willed and mentally challenged youth, and Mary a slut.[17] The inversion is too perfect to provoke anything but a spasm of laughter or horror.

A lesser-known work from Panizza's pen is *The Pig: In Poetic, Mythological, and Moral-historical Perspective* (1900). This brilliantly ludicrous disquisition argues that the 'power and the glory' (1 Chronicles 29:11) belong to a beast. The pig, Panizza claims, is an animal of transcendental significance. In triune majesty, it occupies the place of the Father (the beginning and end of all things), that of the Son (who makes higher reality accessible to mortal reason) and that of the Holy Ghost (connecting the heavenly and earthly realms).

Panizza's reasoning has the elegant simplicity of truth and the seductive pull of mortal sin. The ancient Greeks and Romans associated the pig with generation, specifically the female sexual organs. In contrast, the Egyptians condemned swine and those who tended them. Even if the Jews distanced themselves from their taskmasters, they preserved Egyptian values inasmuch as they forbade the consumption of pork. The corollary of the lawless lust the animal exhibits is the pleasure of communion when eating

it. Even without theological superadditions, the pig *is* carnality –
a 'fleshpot' tying Israel to ignominious servitude. What, then, is
Christianity – a universal faith that knows no distinction between
Jews and Gentiles – but a call for all men to be brothers basking
in the warmth of a new day? '*The Pig is the Sun*', Panizza avers.[18]
He might have written, '*The Pig is the Son*': a Passover meal for
the whole human race.

The modernist gambit reaches beyond the aesthetic sphere,
drawing on scholarly and scientific endeavour. Panizza's thesis
about swine-worship is not much crazier than theories respectable
contemporaries proposed. The first edition of *The Golden Bough*
by J. G. Frazer (1854–1941) appeared in 1890. This far-ranging study
sought to uncover beliefs and practices at the core of the world's
many religions and cultures, including the death and rebirth of
a king alternately revered and sacrificed by the group he ruled.
From Frazer's perspective, the God of monotheistic religion is
the expanded and updated version of the deified local potentates
worshipped by small, primitive tribes. Anthropology posits deep,
abiding structures common to all humankind.

At around the same time, the academic enterprise of sociology
started. In this framework, Émile Durkheim (1858–1917) examined
how religion unifies contradictory and competing interests in the
various forms of human community. Provided that it offers a sense
of direction, a religious system may be based on ancestral totems
or centuries of learned debate; effigies in wood or stone serve the
same purpose as thousands of pages of expert commentary.

But if Panizza's claims reveal points of tangency with the social
sciences, they overlap almost entirely with the project of psychoanalysis initiated by Sigmund Freud (1856–1939). This self-professed
'completely godless Jew' was drawn to everything that confounds

sober reason: sexuality, mental illness and – particularly in later, 'metapsychological' works – religion.[19] In Freud's estimation, life amounts to so many half- to completely misunderstood efforts to master biological drives that, if left unchecked, would leave the human animal rutting and killing in a swamp of filth. The greatest achievements of civilization exist because of prohibitions that keep people from what they really want. Human history stands as a vast gallery of shrines to compromise and frustration. This thoroughly modern intellectual revered tradition, even as he shook its foundations.

In effect, Panizza had all the same obsessions as his contemporary. Whereas Freud did his sober best to steer sex and death towards a (relatively) balanced model of psychic and social order, his zany counterpart took delight in the explosive potential of instinct. The pig, like Jesus Christ, incarnates rupture and continuity between the Old and New Testaments. If Judaism shuns its very presence, Christianity – a 'reform' version of the ancient Law – announces the gospel that the Deity walks and grunts among men, bringing randy vivaciousness and succulent roasts. 'The gift ... hath abounded unto many' (Romans 5:15).

Apocalypses Now

A commonplace of historiography holds that modernization means secularization.[20] Yet as Nietzsche, the son of a Lutheran pastor, shrewdly observed, 'everything profound loves masks'.[21] Illusion is a resource of power, too. Questioning – or deriding – religion does not make it go away. Freud conceded that 'the future of an illusion' looked bright, and Panizza's antics have a carnivalesque quality when viewed against the edifice of Roman

Catholicism. De jure, if not de facto, religion has laid claim to the physical and metaphysical world before any part of the universe comes into being, especially human life. 'Lord, thou art our father; we are the clay, and thou our potter' (Isaiah 64:8).

Religion abides even where it remains invisible. For some two millennia, the Christian faith encouraged concord between 'sons of God' (John 1:12). In the eighteenth century the same set of values found expression in Enlightenment philosophy: it is only natural, if people exercise innate reason and follow sound instinct, for communal life to balance out to general advantage.[22] Subsequently, assorted social movements cultivated and propagated the ideal that 'all men are brothers'; in some cases, provisions were made to include 'sisters' on equal footing.

The opposing yet complementary aspect of 'trickle-down' spirituality is fundamentalism: rigorous adherence to code. Counter to much received opinion, conservatives and even reactionaries need not be motivated by nostalgia. Smart ones see the present for what it is and hate it. Religion provides the means for marching into the future in line with the past, which isn't necessarily better, just more orderly.

The Bible makes it plain that fraternity does not guarantee harmony. Cain kills Abel, Joseph's brothers sell him into slavery, Moses has backsliding followers slain and the Kingdom of Israel and the Kingdom of Judah take up arms against each other. At key junctures, the New Testament adopts a bellicose tone, too. 'Think not that I am come to send peace on earth: I came not to send peace, but a sword. For I am come to set a man at variance against his father . . . And a man's foes shall be they of his own household' (Matthew 10:34–6).[23] 'God with us' (Matthew 1:23) was a battle-cry some 1,500 years before it became a slogan of the German military (*Gott mit uns*).[24] The Book of Revelation envisions war on a universal scale, fought in the name of righteousness.

The Divine Plan foresees much that is not peace and love. If Maistre's 'great law of the spiritual world' ever held, it was truer than ever in what has come to be known as the Great War (1914–18). Prayers and curses followed the bullets, bombs and gas as erstwhile Christendom united in mutual hatred to build a single altar of sacrifice.

Many Europeans welcomed a conflict that cost millions of lives. Overt hostility has the virtue (a word etymologically linked to *vir*, Latin for 'man') of dispelling bad blood, resentment and the simple boredom that poison body and soul. The long-lived Ernst Jünger (1895–1998) describes the mood in *Storm of Steel*: 'We had come from lecture halls, school desks and factory workbenches ... Grown up in an age of security, we shared a yearning for danger, for the experience of the extraordinary.'[25] Desire for adventure offered subjective motivation, but nationalism forged objective masses. The assassination of Archduke Franz Ferdinand, heir presumptive to the sclerotic Austro-Hungarian Empire, sparked the conflict. Dynasties are old, sprawling and full of embarrassing relations. Nations are young and agile, eager to prove themselves.

When the fighting ceased, smoke and fire filled the air. The empires of Great Britain and France started to crumble, the Ottoman Empire abutting the Continent came to an end and a humiliated Germany collapsed into political and economic chaos. Newly founded states dotted the map from the Baltic down to Yugoslavia. In no time at all – at least from a heavenly perspective – all-consuming fires would erupt again. Some scholars call the historical period from 1914 to 1945 the 'Second Thirty Years War.'[26]

Verity knows no expiration date. 'The Lord is a man of war' (Exodus: 15:3). In the modern world, Chosen Peoples marching towards a shared destiny – sovereignty in their own hands, in their own lands – have been as numerous as the 'nations' against which Israel fought in ancient times. And brothers who do not combat each other out in the open will employ ruse and covert violence to obtain their putative birthright.

Apocalyptic declarations flourished before, during and after the Great War.[27] Whether or not people really believed it was all over, and whether or not they found comfort or terror in religion, only the paradigm of revelation could capture what had long started and now was coming to a head. The strangely open end might be imagined literally, figuratively or both. Bad tidings could also presage deliverance: what do the virtuous have to fear?

'The Second Coming' (1919) by William Butler Yeats exemplifies the widespread sense of foreboding. The poet's words are still invoked apropos of every world-shattering crisis, real or imagined.

> Turning and turning in the widening gyre
> The falcon cannot hear the falconer;
> Things fall apart; the centre cannot hold;
> Mere anarchy is loosed upon the world,
> The blood-dimmed tide is loosed, and everywhere
> The ceremony of innocence is drowned;
> The best lack all conviction, while the worst
> Are full of passionate intensity.[28]

On the one hand, the poem is tied to events of recent memory, the First World War. At the same time, the vivid but vague language leaves one free to fill in the blanks about further developments. Prophetic speech, whether divinely inspired or dreamed up by a heretic, opens forwards and backwards at once; it engages the listener, or reader, by capturing the floating state of the day at hand, which hangs suspended between absolutes. Prophecy sounds timely, no matter how often it proves to be wrong.

The last two lines of 'The Second Coming' enjoy particular fame. 'What rough beast, its hour come round at last, / Slouches towards Bethlehem to be born?' It is not the Messiah who is coming again – not yet, anyway – but a 'beast' incubating in the shadows; its entry into life signifies the world's passage into death. The work is addressed to all and sundry, no matter their faith or political alignment. Let them see and do what they will; no one will escape.

Modernist projects that sought to do without God still followed a religious model. The historian Yuri Slezkine has studied the cultural ferment that gave birth to the Russian Revolution (or, more precisely, revolutions) of 1917. 'Most prophets of the Real Day were either Christians or socialists,' he notes, and the two groups viewed each other warily.[29] 'Christians tended to think of socialists as atheists or Antichrists, and socialists tended to agree (while considering Christians backward or hypocritical).' The charged atmosphere had another component, too. A small but vocal number of Jews welcomed a cosmic event that would spell the end of the old regime within their own communities, in Russia as a whole and, ultimately, across the globe. Slezkine brackets questions of what people *thought* they believed. A recruiting Jew looks a lot like a Christian, and Christians who view themselves as 'heirs to a lost sacred mission' sound a lot like Jews. 'The loss of "religious" faith was a prerequisite for spiritual awakening', and 'spiritual awakening' meant political action. The literature, music and visual art of the time – say, the works of Vladimir Mayakovsky (1893–1930) – crackle with metaphysical thrill and dread.[30]

Following decades of confused militancy, clumsy reaction and rampant infighting – not to mention Russia's embarrassing war with Japan, an uprising against the government in 1905, the inadequate reforms that followed and the First World War – it had long seemed the earth would open up and swallow everyone whole; alternatively, the heavens might part and reveal a new and better dispensation. Like a Russian doll, one apocalypse contained many others. The seers vindicated in February 1917, when the Duma (parliament) took over the government, were consigned to the proverbial 'dustbin of history' in October. The Bolsheviks carried the day. For this political sect, inherited religious categories represented mystifications to be discarded as relics of class society and tribal barbarism. The elect were a new people, as augured by dialectical materialism. 'Jewgreek is greekjew. Extremes meet. Death is the highest form of life.'

Fyodor Dostoevsky (1821–1881), who was drawn to radical causes in youth but slouched far to the right in maturity, had seen the storm coming decades earlier. *Notes from Underground* (1864), an exemplar of anti-modern modernism, is written in the voice of a retired civil servant who laments social conditions but entertains no hope for change.

Man really is stupid, phenomenally stupid ... Man, whoever he might be, has always and everywhere liked to act as he wants ... One's own free and voluntary wanting, one's own caprice, however wild, one's own fancy ... Where did all these sages get the idea that man needs some normal, some virtuous wanting? . . . Man needs only *independent* wanting, whatever this independence may cost and wherever it may lead. Well, and this wanting, the devil knows . . .'[31]

Overweening and incoherent self-interest condemns joint endeavours to naught. 'The devil knows' means that people don't have the slightest clue what motivates their '*independent* wanting' – that is, their heretical desires.

Dostoevsky's *Demons*, which appeared some eight years after *Notes from Underground*, explores stupidity on a Promethean scale. Despite the title, nothing supernatural happens over the course of hundreds of pages; introducing actual demons (*besy*) would mean letting people off too easily. The backdrop of the novel is idleness amid too much thinking, drinking and talking: 'innocent, nice, perfectly Russian, liberal chatter.'[32] The parlour jousts of semi-enlightened provincials open an abyss of tragedy and farce. Stepan Trofimovich Verkhovensky, the lapdog of the wealthy Varvara Petrovna Stavrogina and tutor to her son, embodies misguided intellectualism and parental negligence. He gave his own child away to be raised by his aunts. The child, Pyotr, has grown to adulthood and now seeks out his father, bringing along a host of dangerous associates and half-baked schemes for changing the world. Fittingly, events culminate in a literary gala gone awry. In what amounts to a long, dark Walpurgis Night of the soul, the assorted conspirators plunge deeper and deeper into revolutionary delusion until a good part of the town has burned down and half of them are dead.

Dostoevsky's famous pessimism is a form of piety. If people cannot practise Christian virtue, at least they might avoid acting on harebrained schemes. Not everyone heeded the warning. The historical hour – which lasted for decades – belonged to the 'passionate intensity' of heretical optimists riding the 'rough beast' at a full gallop towards a New Jerusalem.

Primeval Modernism

The quest for new horizons could also, paradoxically, look to the remote past. Artists who welcomed a break with the present exulted in theories that upset the age-old view of the cosmos as a pyramid reaching from unshaped matter to celestial perfection.[33] The modern understanding of the world goes from the bottom up, not the top down. Where theologians had spoken of the Fall, a one-time event that yielded an immutable structure, scientists posited an ongoing process. According to Charles Darwin (1809–1882), life forms did not come into being in a completed state – each one 'after its kind', in the biblical phrase. Instead, they emerged in fits and starts; the lucky ones went on to 'be fruitful and multiply'. Creation is still unfolding.[34]

The French philosopher Michel Foucault coined the term 'bio-power' to describe interest in 'the species, descent, and collective welfare' that flourished in scientific, political and economic thinking of the long nineteenth century.[35] Darwin provides just one point of reference. 'Regulating populations'[36] along the lines of health and sickness, wealth and poverty and, most notoriously, racial characteristics stresses the categories of adaptation, function and utility. In this framework, life amounts to a raw material and resource, both an asset and a liability. Like capital, bio-power can be accumulated or squandered; it must always be invested wisely.

In the world of art, Naturalism responded to these developments, inaugurating a major shift in aesthetic criteria and priorities.

Life unbounded: Louis-Henri Brévière, engraving after J. J. Grandville, 'Volvox', illustration in Pierre-Jules Hetzel, pseud. P.-J. Stahl, ed., *Scènes de la vie privée et publique des animaux* (Scenes from the Public and Private Lives of Animals), vol. 1 (1842).

Instead of giving form to ideals and aiming for decorous style, its adherents studied 'facts' and sought to incorporate them into their works, however shocking the results. The movements that emerged in the wake of Naturalism shared its interest in aspects of reality passed over for propriety's sake. Thus Primitivism, Fauvism and Expressionism sought to connect directly with the abiding 'life force' animating the universe. Bold strokes and vibrant splashes of colour held – or tried to hold – the moment of inspiration, 'breath' (*spiritus*) that makes inert matter come alive. Surrealism (that is, 'super-realism', which is almost the same as 'super-naturalism') belongs to this genealogy at one further remove.

In the contiguous realm of literature, writers performed an analogous gesture, excavating lexical minerals with a rare lustre, chopping up syntax into rough-hewn blocks and combining them into verbal mosaics radiating primal energy both physical and metaphysical. Since then, the works of authors of greater and lesser renown have become relics in their own right, monuments to a not-so-distant age that seems to stand worlds apart from our own.

The latter include Gian Pietro Lucini (1867–1914). His poem *For All the Gods Dead and Disowned* (1909) seeks to renew religious experience from the ferment of the modernist swamp. He begins by reimagining the biblical story of origins from the perspective of humanity in its infant state.

> Each clutching the other's hand, the Pair,
> Wound in hides wild and dirty,
> Eyes staring in haunted terror,
> Fled through the tangle of coiled vines,

> Over the slimy knot of serpents,
> Amidst the howls of livid beasts,
> Their mean and menacing companions,
> Across the equinox of the tropics,
> Through strange prehistoric jungles,
> The fiery waste of the storm;
> Savage and human, they, the Pair
> Saw the countenance, monstrous and dreadful,
> Of gold, blood, and flames,
> The face of the nameless Deity
> Through lightning, thunder, and clouds.[37]

Counter to theological doctrine, which declares a spiritual power to be responsible for material creation, Lucini pictures brute matter coupling and combusting in a promiscuous storm; higher forms proceed from lowly elements. God shines forth from inclement weather and muddy ooze, not a burning bush.

The Deity takes form when 'the Pair' try to understand a world bent on destroying them. Anthropology, evolutionary biology and philosophical speculation shed light on a trick of the mind, which Lucini describes in images worthy of Isidore Ducasse, 'Comte de Lautréamont'.

> God, Terror,
> Cause dark and obscure,
> Shot up from lands fatal and fat,
> A shapeless, milky germ of tentacles,
> Mononucleate, slippery polyp,
> Protean in color and shape;
> God, Horror,

> Squat on the tree of the troglodyte age,
> Tall before the green sky of dusk
> Above the waves of the surging deep,
> The bristling of black forests,
> Against caverns battered
> By rain and winds.[38]

God did not create Man as part of a higher plan. Man 'contrived' God in utter panic.[39] A modern initiate into ancient mysteries, Lucini knows the secret names of the Deity: 'Baal, Huitzilopochtli, Jehovah, / God, ruthless God'.[40]

As the work progresses, the poet takes one shot after another at tradition and orthodoxy. Invoking the New Testament expression 'fishers of men' (Matthew 4:19), he writes: 'Fortune's yours . . . Jewish fisherman, / Who knew to sink, at the right hour, / Traps dark and strong . . . / Into the very heart of the Roman world'.[41] Similar examples abound. The Church represents a pirate vessel embarked on a 'deceitful voyage lasting centuries'. Inherited beliefs and practices amount to superstition, at best.

Yet Lucini's purposes are not simply iconoclastic. His readings in classical philology yield modern mythology, his consultation of scientific writings leads to quasi-religious certainty, and looking backwards shows him how to move forwards. Ultimately, the poet announces a kind of Pentecostal gift.

> For us, the Mystery lies within,
> Inside the boundless shudder
> That pulls, judges, and rejects,
> The exalted frenzy

> Of all the senses, the fibers of our flesh,
> The vitality that rouses speech and passion,
> Making us bite fast and beg, die and be reborn,
> The Hidden Deity revealed in every pulse.
> God lies in Us,
> Like a holy vessel of Might.[42]

The 'Hidden Deity' dwells and swells in the human breast, a force primeval and eternal at once, rising and falling, now and forever. *For All the Gods Dead and Disowned* is an apocalypse in the original sense of the word: the 'uncovering' of transcendental truth.[43]

Although a minor prophet, Lucini belonged to an international chorus of heretics tearing at the canon, received notions and conventional style in order to 'make it new', as Ezra Pound memorably put the matter. Hence the efforts of Gertrude Stein to infuse 'the excitingness of pure being' back into language, so it might now sparkle as it once did for Chaucer and Homer,[44] when the heavens and earth still lay closer together. Hence, also, the volcanic eruptions of Antonin Artaud, who, hag-ridden by the 'exalted frenzy' of nervous sensation, would have liked nothing more than to flush the material world (and with it, God, his tormentor) down a black hole.[45]

Germany brought forth its own versions of the 'Mystery . . . within'. One of the most captivating explorations comes from Gottfried Benn (1886–1956), a doctor whose expertise in dermatological conditions and venereal diseases gave his jaundiced view of the world a gruesome vividness. A hint of infamy clings to Benn because he joined the National Socialist party, even though it didn't take long for him to fall out of favour with a movement

No God and no Devil: Rolf von Hoerschelmann, cover illustration for *Morgue* (1923) by Gottfried Benn.

that prized clean living. Given the nature of his works, disrepute suits him better than most.

A morbid sensibility does not preclude verve. 'Urgesicht' (1928) provides an object lesson in what Nietzsche had called the 'pessimism of strength'. The title may be translated either as 'primal vision', in the sense of a thing beheld, or as 'primal sight', in which case it refers to the faculties of the beholder. As in *For All the Gods Dead and Disowned*, revelation signifies vitalism 'beyond good and evil'.

Benn's poem in prose offers an account of the 'epic of an instant' that seizes an unnamed narrator (presumably the author himself) on a day 'without anything special about it' at the 'beginning of November', as the seasons slowly turn.[46] Amid recollections of country outings and views from an urban apartment that is 'high above everything', the speaker experiences what his contemporary Walter Benjamin, in a different but related context, called 'profane illumination': mystical transport bursting forth out of a disenchanted and colourless world.

The language races as fast as thought itself through decades, centuries and aeons. Intermittently spiralling outwards again to earlier epochs, the 'return of times' (*Wiederkehr der Zeiten*) circle back to the present day, hour, minute and second. Finally, 'the myth that began in Babylon' takes shape in a jitterbugging parade:

Uniform idols, schemata in drilled choreography, standard-issue goods, worship under spotlights, communion with jazz, Gethsemane as the record for ecstasy, Christ the successful entrepreneur, socialite, advertising genius, and founder of modern business . . . The dollar was willed by God, property ownership is inherently ethical; hence Bible lessons against drops in the market . . . The New World's prophet of 'Keep Smiling!' The new type: with his stigmata, he marks the earth: the suspension bridge from Manhattan to Fort Lee, which will be done in 1932 – 1067 meters long, supported by four cables, each one 914 millimeters in diameter.[47]

The nauseous vision eclipses all else in a neon glare. Words, which at least promise meaning, give way to more and more numbers: calculations that wash away the past. The dawning 'American Century' amounts to a cult of mass-manufactured idols. The scene is a Teutonic version of 'The Waste Land' (1922) or 'The Hollow Men' (1925) by T. S. Eliot.

> *This is the way the world ends*
> *This is the way the world ends*
> *This is the way the world ends*
> *Not with a bang but a whimper.*[48]

The gospel of technological advancement and commerce have paved over the earth and drowned out the music of the spheres.

Yet the seer does not succumb to despair. Even as cacophony and vulgarity run rampant, an obscure pulse – 'rhythmical monism' – throbs away.[49] In time, he grows calm and experiences 'clarity beyond compare'. The constellations formed by enduring signs beyond the smoke and mirrors point to a vast, cosmic cycle. Ultimately, the whirling dance of impressions coalesce into a kind of animate hieroglyph:

I saw the *I*, the look out of its eyes, I widened its pupil, looked deep inside, looked out from deep within, the gaze from such eyes . . . sensing danger, an ancient danger. Out of catastrophes . . . horrendous memories of the race, double-sexed, animal-formed, bent over like a sphinx [*grauenvolle*

Erinnerungen des Geschlechts, Zwitterhaftes, Tiergestaltiges, Sphinxgebeuteltes] . . . I recalled strange pronouncements, that one should give up seeking those last words, whose sound, if ever voiced, would make the Earth shake.[50]

Here, encountering the other 'I', the poet's alter ego communes with an *alter* alter ego. This experience of a dilated moment opens onto another plane of reality, beyond the trash of a flat and fatuous world.

In the unblinking gaze of something like Lucini's God – a 'Mononucleate, slippery polyp, / Protean in color and shape' – the debris of millennia of civilization and the empty temples of the modern desert cease to provoke revulsion. The seer basks in delectation as part of a greater, more authentic and more primordial power.

> I stood and listened. For a long time, I stood and breathed the sound. Life wanted to preserve itself, but Life also wanted to perish . . .
> And above everything, unconsciousness and dream . . . Ancient transformations, twilight and poppies, down the ladder, to the murmur of distant waters.[51]

This private apocalypse might seem chilling, but it connotes warmth, like a mother's milk. Few may nurse at the teat of a sphinx, but those who can are the elect. Instead of ascending to the heavens, the visionary climbs 'down the ladder' – of evolution, no doubt – to commune with the Alpha and Omega that whisper blissful doom: 'unconsciousness and dream' from which one need never awake.

Poor Devils

Europe and North America would have benefited from a little more satanic rigour in the run-up to the great catastrophes of the twentieth century. An unconventional work of Christian apologetics by C. S. Lewis, *The Screwtape Letters*, appeared during the Second World War, when 'the widening gyre' had reached terminal velocity. In this surprisingly good-natured satire, a nominal agent of evil affirms the soundness of God's Creation.

Screwtape, a senior bureaucrat of the underworld, offers advice to his nephew Wormwood, who is trying to harvest a soul for Satan, 'Our Father'. The avuncular fiend observes that people are 'half spirit and half animal':

As spirits they belong to the eternal world, but as animals they inhabit time. This means that while their spirit can be directed to an eternal object, their bodies, passions, and imaginations are in continual change, for to be in time means to change. Their nearest approach to constancy, therefore, is undulation – the repeated return to a level from which they repeatedly fall back, a series of troughs and peaks.[52]

The picture of hapless, swimming creatures parallels the one that 'Lautréamont' describes in *Les chants de Maldoror*, minus the filthy imagery and crushing atmosphere of doom. 'Humans are amphibians.' More importantly, it is in keeping with Augustinian theology that mortals inhabit a 'region of dissimilarity' by nature, and it agrees with the position of the medieval Church, according to which people are drawn upwards and downwards simultaneously by nobler and baser components of their being.

For Lewis, as for his non-modernist forebears, devils have a job to do, and they aren't very good at it. The problem is that they resemble their prey, with 'bodies, passions, and imaginations' subject to 'continual change'. Wormwood is always flying from one scheme to the next and botching his work. Screwtape, although he is more competent, runs into trouble, too. At one point, he gets carried away and finds that he has 'inadvertently . . . assume[d] the form of a large centipede'; the rest of the missive must be dictated to a secretary, a certain 'Toadpipe'. Infernal functionaries are just like human beings, only worse. They *really* can't stop changing.

In other words, devils embody unchecked vitality. Even the more intelligent among them cannot escape hyperactivity. Embarrassed, Screwtape tries to cover for his metamorphosis with sententious commentary, observing that 'the poet Milton' and other old-fashioned authors have understood 'such changes of shape [as] a "punishment"'. In contrast, the new generation knows better. 'A more modern writer – someone with a name like Pshaw – has . . . grasped the truth. Transformation proceeds from within and is a glorious manifestation of that Life Force which Our Father would worship if he worshipped anything but himself.' The 'truth' grasped by George Bernard Shaw, author of *Man and Superman*, is what fuels works by Lucini, Benn and any number of their peers. The 'Life Force' prized by modern heretics and poor devils is a 'germ of tentacles' without shape, definition or direction, demanding obedience without issuing orders at all. Screwtape might as well be hiding under a rock, fitfully dreaming of the quiet 'murmur of distant waters' with Nazis and other go-getters. He and his kind will never know rest.

Lewis's perspective is fusty, but not gloomy. For human beings, the 'troughs and peaks' of existence need not be so choppy.

People might want for positive virtue, but they have negative potential. Unlike the paper-pushers and errand boys of Hell, they can calm down. What's the rush? They've done plenty already, and they'll be dead soon enough.

EIGHT

A Satanic Symphony

According to the Bible, both Hebrew and Christian, Satan performs a God-given function. Secular literature, we have seen, assigns him much the same role. Our examination of a rich and varied body of works in many languages and from different periods of history has made the case for acquitting the Adversary of many of the charges levelled against him. Indeed, Satan is exempt from prosecution because he *is* the prosecution.

Yet confusion persists. Most people see the Adversary as the source of ills that in fact derive from men and women's own wickedness or represent a test approved by the Deity. Such a biased view is unlikely to go away, because it affords a convenient means for sinners to escape responsibility. This final chapter broadens the perspective by looking at notes struck on the human instrument. Satan's musical skill matches his abilities in the verbal arena. No matter how strange it may sound, the Devil plays by the rules here, too.

Concord and Discord

The first occurrence of music in the Bible is paradigmatic. After their Egyptian pursuers have perished, Moses and the children of Israel intone a hymn:

> The Lord is my strength and song, and he is become my salvation: he is my God ... my father's God, and I will exalt him.
>
> ...
>
> Pharaoh's chariots and his host hath he cast into the sea: his chosen captains also are drowned in the Red sea.
>
> The depths have covered them: they sank into the bottom as a stone (Exodus 15:2–5).

These chanted words, offered to God at the fulfilment of collective destiny, represent a spontaneous outpouring of relief and gratitude. The glory of the moment does not last, however. The Israelites' wanderings before reaching the Promised Land will witness the death of Moses and his generation. Music means escape, yet the deliverance it celebrates and manifests is passing. 'The people ... thou hast purchased' (Exodus 15:16) have been freed from Egyptian slavery to become bondsmen of the Lord with further work to do. Divine 'mercy' (Exodus 15:13) means that the elect will turn from patients to agents, charged with performing on others the same violence they have suffered.[1] The campaign will be clamorous and bloody.

David, the model Jewish ruler, commands the art of song. Music, like political might, is not wholly of this earth. The psalms, many of which he is supposed to have written, ensure order by lending a single articulate voice to the flock, lest members stray and bleat fractiously. Power wielded by singing and playing the harp guides royal subjects more gently than the ram's horn blown by 'the sons of Aaron, the priests', appointed in the Book of Numbers to assemble the masses in peace and war (10:8).

Music of praise endured as Christianity emerged from Judaism, but its otherworldly force also inspired misgiving. Augustine, for example, harboured doubts about using song in worship because 'the general experience of the senses is . . . lust', and music is so sweet.[2] If the great theologian believed that 'our souls . . . are more religiously and with a warmer devotion kindled to piety' when 'sacred words are chanted well', he recognized that such magic can obscure the holy message and spirit listeners away.[3] Etymologically, *music* derives from the Greek *mousikē*. The word refers to the Muses, goddesses presiding over the arts and sciences. Daughters of Zeus, the supreme god of the ancient pantheon, they are led by Mnemosyne, the divine embodiment of memory. The very idea has something pagan about it, suggesting the enticements and lures of self-renewing nature. Augustine saw the risks clearly: music elevates and exalts, but it can also leave mortals hanging in a realm more carnal than spiritual, ready to fall.

Still, the early history of Christian music was calm and the bonds it wove delicate. Monastic communities made liturgical chants an integral part of life in service to God, and shared worship structured the passing of hours. In services attended by the laity, hymns performed the same function: holy communion overcame the pains of the 'region of dissimilarity' that men and women otherwise inhabit.[4] Today, the Gregorian chants that crowned the first millennium of Christianity express the same sentiments and spirituality, affording refuge from chaos and strife.

Only in the heavens does the music last forever. Down on earth, dangers abound, and it takes keen senses and an alert mind to discern them. This is where the Devil, who specializes in false signs and misdirection, steps in to make trial of mortals. The Adversary made his musical debut by offering a dissonant counterpoint to harmony in *Ordo virtutum* (The Order of Virtues) by the Benedictine abbess Hildegard of Bingen (1098–1179), known to posterity as the 'Sibyl of the Rhine' for her visions, writings and compositions.[5]

The first morality play by over a century, *Ordo virtutum* features an allegorical cast. The protagonist is 'Soul', *Anima*. Though happy at first, Anima comes to despair that she has a body and must endure earthly vicissitudes before basking in the eternal light. As she steers her course through our vale of tears, she faces temptation and trial. The Adversary – *Diabolus* – intrudes and derides divine promises. 'What is this power – as if there were no one but God?'[6] he asks the pilgrim with a sneer. Such unmusical interjections are not cast in meter. Diabolus disrupts the singing with speech that does not mean anything inasmuch as its purpose is to obstruct words floating heavenwards. Ugly form mirrors cacophonous content. Rushing to the pilgrim's aid, the personified Virtues – Hope, Humility, Mercy, Modesty and so on – take the stage. In dulcet tones, they urge Anima to cling to her resolve. The contrast could not be stronger. Noble qualities are metrical and godly; Diabolus brings forth only joyless noise.

With help from higher faculties sent from the skies, Anima prevails. The pageant concludes with Chastity declaring – in lovely song, of course – that the Adversary has been undone and life's challenges overcome. The wording is important. Only now, when the battle is decided, does the name 'Satan' – *Satanas* – occur.

> In the mind of the Highest, Satan, I trod on your
> > head [*caput*],
> And in a virgin form I nurtured a sweet miracle
> When the Son of God came into the world;
> Therefore you are laid low, with all your plunder;
> And now let all who dwell in heaven rejoice,
> Because your belly [*venter*] has been confounded.[7]

So long as Anima was still making her way towards God, the voice of opposition was identified as belonging to Diabolus – a word that, we may recall, means 'slanderer'.[8] Satanas names the personified principle at the antipodes of heaven, the *essence* that commands *accidents* on the earth.[9] Diabolical hindrances manifest this primordial power on a secondary level, which is still too much for mortal souls to take on their own.

Diabolus stands for empirical obstacles and weakness, such as attend creaturely existence. His 'slanders' are the inherent flaws that riddle being, the assorted compounds constituting nature. He is physical – a force circulating in the material universe. The Devil shows up uninvited, but he has every right to do so: the body represents part of nature, and thus this realm is his home, too. Fittingly, almost the first word that Diabolus utters is '*Ego*'.[10] Mortal life is alienated within itself: Anima is distressed because the stirrings she experiences are both intimate and foreign.

Satanas represents the deep aspect of what Diabolus incarnates. The lower realm, which inverts and parodies the harmony of the heavens, is where he has his seat. *Venter* signifies physical lust and craving: the fleshly desires that the Devil expresses so crudely. When Chastity declares, 'I trod on your head . . . your belly has been confounded,' she is upending an upended arrangement, restoring psychic and cosmic balance. *Caput* should connect to the realm of immaterial Ideas, not form part of the gastrointestinal tract. Once laid low by active virtue, the Adversary no longer projects a voice imperilling salvation in either an essential or an accidental capacity.

Ordo virtutum pre-dates the *Divine Comedy* by well over a century and *Canterbury Tales* by at least twice as much time. However, Hildegard's cosmology agrees with the order evident in the works of Dante and Chaucer. Diabolism circulates with relative freedom, for it corresponds to the inherent defectiveness of material creation – which includes, at the summit of 'perfect imperfection', the human soul, ever seeking something better. The satanic dimension, from which the devilry plaguing mortal existence derives, lies outside of time – at the other end of eternity, as it were, far from supernal music.

Dante's Satan says nothing, nor does Chaucer's Sathanas. According to the medieval worldview, there would be no point for the 'fully realized' Adversary in Hell to speak: in his domain, beyond human experience and comprehension, whatever he might say would fade before the truth on high – which mortal intelligence cannot compute, either. Hildegard, who was celebrated for her theological subtlety and mystical insight, paints the same picture. Ultimately, Satan is an unruly element made to serve order. Consigned to a determinate location, even chaos plays a role in the divine plan.

The Adversary in both his capacities had no song to sing during the Middle Ages. Life lived under his mournful wing really is a mistake. The Devil offers cacophonous verbal gas: disquiet for the human soul to overcome by maintaining pious resolve and steering an unwavering course. Satan, the metaphysical version of the Devil, is simply mute. In *Ordo virtutum,* whatever he might still announce is eclipsed first by Chastity's song, then by her sisters' joyful hymn soaring aloft:

> Almighty Father, from you flowed a fountain in fiery
>   love:
> Guide your children into a fair wind, sailing the
>   waters,
> So that we too may steer them in this way
> Into the heavenly Jerusalem.[11]

The point merits emphasis: these words are sung, and in unison. The verses match up with their message, like one element pouring – and turning – into another. Just as the 'fiery love' of the 'Almighty Father' does not burn but yields a 'fountain', the chorus's voices magically shift from sound to vision: the irenic apocalypse of a journey guided by 'fair wind' to 'Jerusalem' in the skies.

The mouth of Hell may have gaped wide in the Middle Ages, but its roar meant nothing more than the crash and din of waves breaking on the shore. The singing in *Ordo virtutum,* already pleasing, heralds song more wondrous still, for all that belongs to the earth must wax and wane. Compared to immortal perfection, even the greatest achievements of this world vanish like stars at sunrise.

Up in Arms

According to a philosophical tradition going back to antiquity, good music helps to fashion good people. This is why Plato's *Republic* extols this art, properly employed, as a prelude to 'gymnastic', the physical counterpart of spiritual exercise, for the guardians of the state.[12] Music coordinates bodies, which otherwise just mill about, and minds, which tend to wander. Jewish tradition acknowledges the same principle. 'The Lord shall reign for ever and ever' (Exodus 15:18), Moses and his followers sing. By manifesting devotion in this way, a people lost in the desert rallies and prevails against a more numerous foe; as heirs to the Jews' sacred mission, Christians follow their lead. A signal of submission to divine will, music also represents discipline and determination.

In the medieval cosmos, the musical canon – a composition that goes round and round like the heavens above – echoed the canonization of saints, the Church's recognition of the rare human life that merits repeating. Its chiming quality intimated that all is not lost in the temporal world; the peace of the afterlife may intermittently prevail, even here. The moments of self-loss that music induces, fleeting but happy instants of self-extinction, portend transport to come. Singing abounds in Dante's *Paradiso*, and the sonorous airs of the poet's words match the figures and themes they announce. When the inhabitants of celestial mansions address the pilgrim, they do so intoning hymns. On high, God commands an eternal 'wheel' that draws the poet's soul onwards and upwards with harmony for the eyes and ears alike.[13] In contrast, *Inferno* features visions and noises that inspire only flight – as when one of the Malebranche makes a 'trumpet' of his rectum.[14]

Notwithstanding the changes it brought, the Reformation preserved this aspect of Catholic culture. Martin Luther held music in great esteem, noting that 'Satan is very hostile to it, since it casts out ... evil thoughts.'[15] By means of music, even mortal minds may apprehend God's intelligent design:

The Devil can make a racket: Erhard Schön,
Demon Playing Monk Bagpipe, c. 1535, satirical print.

> When man's natural musical ability is whetted and polished
> to the extent that it becomes an art, then . . . [we note] the
> great and perfect wisdom of God in music . . . we marvel when
> we hear music in which one voice sings a simple melody,
> while three, four, or five other voices play and . . . adorn [it],
> thus reminding us of a heavenly dance, where all meet in a
> spirit of friendliness.

The Wittenberg reformer continues: 'A person who gives this some thought and yet does not regard it as a marvelous creation of God . . . does not deserve to be called a human being; he should be permitted to hear nothing but the braying of asses and the grunting of hogs.'[16] Music animates the letter of the law that governs the universe, revealing its living spirit. Its quality is rhetorical – not in the degraded sense of 'verbal manipulation', but in the sense of artfully arranged elements, which induce willingness to think, feel and act in accordance with a greater plan. As Dietrich Bartel notes, Luther's 'emphasis on preaching the Word in . . . services' fits seamlessly with his conception of music.[17] 'Simple melody' inviting 'three, four, or five other voices [to] play and . . . adorn [it]' offers an image of ideal predication: concentric rings propagating the Gospel abroad.

Luther wanted song to ring out all over Christendom, yet 'joyful noise unto the Lord' did not mean just sweetness and light. When he declared that music 'makes people happy' because it 'drives away the Devil', Luther also had combat in mind.[18] Without the comfort of indulgences, saintly intercession, Marian mercy and the other trappings of Catholic 'superstition', human existence threatens unremitting tribulation and trial. Accordingly, true believers must steel themselves for a fight.

Inasmuch as Protestantism dismantled the metaphysical architecture erected by Catholic theology, the Adversary acquired freedom of movement and speech. With earthiness befitting his peasant stock, Luther claimed he could drive him away by farting.[19] The hymns he composed, though more agreeable to the senses, pursued the same objective. Take, for instance, his reworking of Psalm 46, which begins:

> A mighty fortress is our God,
> A bulwark never failing [*ein gute Wehr und Waffen*];
> Our helper He, amid the flood
> Of mortal ills prevailing . . .

So far, the meaning of the source is preserved: the Lord is all-powerful, and the protection He offers certain. But the verses that follow head in a new direction:

> For still our ancient foe [*Der alte böse Feind*]
> Doth seek to work us woe;
> His craft and power are great,
> And, armed with cruel hate,
> On earth is not his equal.
> . . .
> And though this world, with devils filled,
> should threaten to undo us,
> We will not fear, for God hath willed
> His truth to triumph through us.[20]

The biblical text makes no reference to an infernal horde; the Tanakh knows nothing of evil armies that are not human. Luther, on the other hand, presents a vision of the world teeming with devils. The gates of Hell now stand wide open. Not only is Satan again 'going to and fro in the earth', he commands forces that are laying siege to bastions of piety. As the sixteenth- and seventeenth-century wars of religion soon proved, this was no metaphor.[21]

Were it not for the promise of deliverance, the hymn would express a death wish:

> Let goods and kindred go,
> This mortal life also;
> The body they may kill:
> God's truth abideth still . . .

The words both evoke a mythical time of foundation and herald the end of days. The exhortation to 'strive' continuously against the assaults of wickedness all but calls for martyrdom – and shedding the blood of others. The flipside of the Christian renewal the reformer promises is nail-biting paranoia.

> The Prince of Darkness [*der Fürst dieser*
>   *Welt*] grim,
> We tremble not for him;
> His rage we can endure,
> For lo, his doom is sure . . .

If this declaration is true, it is so only to the extent that righteous Christian soldiers swear by, and heed, every military order. 'We tremble not' and 'his doom is sure' express wishes more than they represent statements of fact. What is translated as 'the Prince of Darkness' is actually 'the Prince of this World' in the German.

Instead of an unchanging design where all beings have an appointed place, Protestantism descried a universe where what conforms to the Divine Plan is comparatively infrequent and threatened. During the Middle Ages Satan had been banished to the pit. From here, his associates might work their way into the company of mortals, but diabolical activity actually guaranteed that things would follow their proper course; spiritual work left undone might still be completed in Purgatory. Only thoroughly rotten souls were thought to fall from the Tree of Life forever. In contrast, reformed Christians envisioned a garden ready to run wild with shoots, vines and weeds. Any spot lighted by Heaven was bordered by shadows no sun ever reached. Salvation is a hard-won reward, to be achieved through constant cutting, clearing and construction.

In war combatants operate both directly and by stealth, and it can be difficult to know when an attack is coming. Decades before writing *Paradise Lost*, John Milton composed a Puritanical version of *Ordo virtutum*. The allegorical *Mask Presented at Ludlow Castle, 1634* revisits the age-old theme of imperiled chastity and antici-pates the poet's later epic of the Fall. It has come to be known as *Comus*, after the 'damn'd wizard' who would lead the innocent to perdition.[22]

The actual protagonist of *Comus* is an unnamed 'Lady' lost in the 'Dim darkness' of the forest; her two brothers have wan-dered off in search of 'Berries, or such cooling fruit' to refresh themselves and her for the remaining journey.[23] Whatever the siblings may think, 'the kind hospitable Woods' teem with danger.[24] Disguised as a 'gentle villager', Comus – son of the pagan deity Bacchus and the witch Circe – appears before the young woman.[25] Claiming to 'know each lane, and every alley green, / Dingle or bushy dell' of the 'wild' terrain, he proposes to take her to his abode and supply victuals to restore her. One false move and she finds herself trapped in her escort's lair – as the author describes it, '*a stately Palace set out with all manner of deliciousness; soft Music, Tables spread with all dainties*.'[26] Here, the 'unblest enchanter vile' would induce her to take a bite of the apple.[27]

Hildegard made devilish craft noisy and ugly. Milton represents it as seductive and alluring. The difference between their visions reflects the change in how Catholics and Protestants understood Creation and humankind's place within it. For the Roman Church, the various parts of God's world add up to something better and better, until Ultimate Good crowns it all; evil and sin are real, but they represent exceptions to the abiding rule of Providence. For Reformed Christianity, the world is a much flatter place: a 'Labyrinth' where errant souls need to hack and saw to stay on the proper course; in this tangle, an enemy may sound like a friend.[28] The individual believer, just like the community of the Christian elect, cannot afford not to exercise vigilance for even a moment.

By abolishing mediating instances between humankind and the supernatural realm, Reformed Christianity left the faithful to confront dangers directly. Diabolical figures – if not the very Devil – circulated more freely than ever. Now, each waking hour potentially threatened one's eternal soul. In the words of the historian Darren Oldridge, Satan transformed 'into a central actor in daily life', lurking in corners just beyond the compass of the conscious mind.[29]

The conflict in *Comus* achieves resolution by a telling combination of action and inaction. The heroine possesses a 'hidden strength': 'no goblin or swart Faëry / Hath hurtful power over true virginity'.[30] This virtue is largely passive, however. On the 'venom'd seat / Smear'd with gums of glutinous heat' where she sits bound, the captive parries her would-be seducer's thrusts, but she gains no ground.[31] Finally, swords drawn, her brothers liberate her from her captor; they have recognized the menace she faces only because Milton has included a beneficent 'Attendant Spirit' in the cast. This figure, who is as much an angel as Comus is a devil, watches over the travellers and sees to it that the wrongs his fiendish counterpart perpetrates are held in check. Little room exists for human beings to *do* anything: clinging to belief and miracles will happen – if a higher power so wills.

Comus commands '*a rout of Monsters headed like sundry sorts of wilde Beasts, but otherwise like Men and Women*', people who have drunk from his cup and, like the companions of Odysseus bewitched by Circe, turned into animals.[32] The 'braying of asses and the grunting of hogs' never sounded so good. The 'tread / Of hateful steps' dances to a merry song, and a pagan orgy nearly tramples chastity underfoot.[33] Milton started his romance with the 'Devil's party' at an early date. The lady's honour is preserved, but not by much more than a hair.

Diabolus in Musica

Medieval devils gadding about might have chattered and connived, but their sport mirrored their victims' folly; it never achieved eloquence on a grand scale. Satan himself might have occasionally thundered, but his noxious emissions did not amount to discourse; in essence, if not in fact, he was mute. From the Reformation on, in contrast, the Adversary displayed winning ways: power of speech and rhetorical refinement as elaborate as the subtlest heresies. Milton all but made him sing. This change corresponded to divisions within Christendom: Roman Catholicism of varying degrees of orthodoxy, on the one hand, and pullulating Protestant sects, on the other. Christianity now included opposing viewpoints that were equally articulate – which, depending on the side taken, counted as dangerous, seductive and satanic.

The corollary of Satan's command of language and argument corresponded to a newfound presence in music. Traditionally, composers hewed to a pious register, avoiding the *tritone* because of its restless and foreboding effects.[34] This interval, three whole tones in sequence left hanging, opens a space of uncertainty that reflects and induces tension. Since at least the early eighteenth century, it has been known as *diabolus in musica*, 'the devil in music'. Although the tritone occurs in music of the Baroque and Classical periods – for example, in Bach's cantatas, or to convey Leporello's fear that he is facing a demon in Mozart's *Don Giovanni* – here it performs a subordinate role, adding counterpoint or accent before harmonious order is restored.

As we have seen, the Devil's literary career flourished in the nineteenth century. From Byron to Baudelaire and beyond, self-styled poetic Satanists explored the heights and depths of spiritual experience loosed from dogmatic strictures. Such devilry had a pendant in music – for instance, parts of Franz Liszt's *Dante Sonata* (1849). Passages in a minor key riddled with suspenseful tritones underscore the infernal setting – in contrast to sequences in a major key and wholesome intervals, which convey the joy of souls in heaven. Like a serpentine seducer, the 'devil in music' did not crash onto the stage; instead, it insinuated itself into Edenic settings, gathering out of brighter, more placid airs like shadow or fog.

Music's supernatural power and the figure of the tortured genius converged in the self-representations of Romanticism. The foremost representative is E.T.A. Hoffmann (1776–1822), the master of fantasy and horror; his alter ego, *Kapellmeister* Johannes Kreisler, is the very type of the musician who lives half in reality, half in a universe of wild fancy. In France the vividness of his style inspired Jacques Offenbach (1819–1880) to make the artist himself the protagonist of an opera, *The Tales of Hoffmann* – as if events the author made up had happened to him personally. The mad composer is the double of the visionary poet. The exceptional individual experiences the movements of history and cosmos alike. A refined sensibility reveals the full scope of universal emotions and psychic states; the blessing, which is also a curse, allows the artist to feel, and give form to, higher and deeper dimensions of human existence in general.

Thomas Mann's novel *Doctor Faustus* (1947) enlists Romantic tradition to draw parallels between personal misfortune and worldwide disaster. In full, the wilfully anachronistic title reads, *Doctor Faustus: The Life of the German Composer Adrian Leverkühn, Told by a Friend.* The words hearken back to the time when the Faust legend originated: the end of the Middle Ages and the beginning of the wars of religion that followed the Reformation. The word used for 'composer', *Tonsetzer*, means 'tone-setter'. It conjures up a coarse, woodcut world, when *Germania* was still being hewn from the rough elements of even earlier times. *Leverkühn* identifies the protagonist as a man who lives (*leben*) boldly, even to the point of hubris (*kühn*). The composer has been marked from birth. *Nomen est omen.* His story reflects an age as grim as any other period of history, if not worse.

Like Mann's other works, *Doctor Faustus* displays impressive erudition. A modern counterpart to the medieval *summa*, the book seeks to take in and commentate the whole of human knowledge. As a work of fiction, the novel explores how individuals embody and come to terms (or fail to come to terms) with conflicted conditions of life. A friend, one Serenus Zeitblom, tells the composer's story. As the narrator's Christian name suggests, Serenus is calm and reflective. *Zeitblom* identifies him as a child of the modern world (literally, a 'flower of the times'). This character is the antithesis of his tempestuous contemporary but his dialectical complement, as well: a plodding accountant whose horoscope has placed him alongside a racing comet of a man. Zeitblom knows a lot, but he does not always understand it.

Mann modelled Leverkühn's technique on that of real-life composer Arnold Schoenberg (1874–1951).[35] He also found

The Devil can play the best tunes: Louis-Léopold Boilly, 'Tartini's Dream', 1824, lithograph of the legend behind Giuseppe Tartini's 'Devil's Trill Sonata'.

inspiration in countless other figures of recent German history, including Oswald Spengler (1880–1936). In his massive *Decline of the West*, which appeared in two volumes during and after the First World War, Spengler had sought to make Nietzsche's 'outlook' into an 'overlook' by identifying three grand-scale cycles of history that swell and fade like Wagnerian music dramas.[36] Modern times, he declared, represent the 'Faustian' epoch; Europe has attained the point once achieved by the 'Apollonian' and 'Magian' ages, which were centred in the ancient Greek and medieval Arab worlds, respectively. These cultures thrived as much as their native genius permitted but then, following cosmic laws of growth and decay, lapsed into decadence. Spengler presents an ambivalent view of his own historical moment: on the one hand, modern accomplishments cannot be denied; on the other hand, the 'Living Time' that commands the world has doomed European civilization to extinction.[37] Just as Nature wipes away species, History buries peoples.

Mann weaves myriad strands of past and present together to dramatize the moment when Zeitblom tells his cautionary tale. The novel unfolds retrospectively, extending from the late nineteenth century to the time of its writing. No reader can fail to remark the political allegory, especially inasmuch as the allotted span of Leverkühn's career extends from the end of the First World War to the early stage of the Second. However, Mann does not directly equate Hitler, National Socialism or the Second World War – all of which his narrator views with horror – with the eruption of metaphysical evil, nor does he blame the Adversary for these events. Instead, over the course of more than five hundred pages, *Doctor Faustus* orchestrates voices as varied as the human actors on the world stage. Some of them are delicate and soft; others are strident and piercing. Nationalists boom and pacifists whimper; the discourses of reedy intellectuals combine with the war-march of politicians. Recurring phrases and slogans grate against finely wrought eloquence. Leverkühn stands at the centre of a surge of waves that ultimately engulf him, like a conductor trying to command the elements by waving a wooden baton.

Where, like his namesake in Marlowe and Goethe, the twentieth-century 'Faustus' taps into powers beyond mortal control, Satan emerges in counterpoint: a presence between the lines whispering notes that advance the piece's movement but never coalesce into a harmonious balance. In fact, the narrative leaves it up in the air whether the Tempter really exists, even in the fiction. The prosaic Zeitblom never encounters him, and Leverkühn, a mad genius, dwells too much in a realm of pathological fantasy to be credible. The composer has actively contracted syphilis from a prostitute in order to magnify his receptivity to inspiration. He claims to have met the Devil, but his word is hardly to be trusted. It is certain, however, that Temptation exists – and that Leverkühn embraces it.

German philosophy has a tradition of holding music in high regard. According to Arthur Schopenhauer (1788–1860), music represents the highest form of expression because it manifests the Will most purely. With voluble understatement, Mann notes that 'the Devil surely knows something' of the art at which the Teutonic tribes have excelled in modern times.[38] Though 'cosmopolitan at heart', Satan is 'German to the core' in the Faustian Age. He changes form throughout his meeting with Leverkühn, but still proves 'old and familiar' enough to elicit occasional laughter.[39] The composer is the spiritual kinsman of 'the true Lord of Enthusiasm'.[40]

The key word is 'enthusiasm', which concerns quantity above quality: the 'reeling whirl . . . the most painful excess, / Enamored hate and quickening distress', as Goethe's Faust put it a century and a half earlier. The advocate of 'emancipated art', Satan represents unbridled creativity.[41] A sinister optimist, he deems it 'slander' to be equated with 'criticism'.[42] Now as ever, Satan exploits human desires that are already there. The gifts of the twentieth-century 'Faustus' do not exempt him from the human condition. If anything, they make matters worse.

Addressing Leverkühn in the 'royal we', 'the untransmogrified Sammael' makes a proposal:

We pledge to you the vital efficacy needed for what you will accomplish with our help. You will lead, you will set the march for the future, lads will swear by your name . . . In their health they will gnaw at your madness, and you will become healthy in them. Do you understand? It is not merely that you will break through the laming difficulties of the age – you will break through the age itself . . . and dare . . . barbarism . . . Believe me, barbarism has a better understanding even of theology than does a culture that has fallen off from the cult, which even in things religious saw only culture, only humanitarianism, but not excess, not the paradox, the mystical passion, the ordeal so utterly outside bourgeois experience.[43]

As per the classic agreement, Leverkühn will receive 24 years of service. The wording is significant. The composer's secret sharer speaks the language of the avant-garde. Mann's Satan is not only modern; he's a modernist. Leverkühn will escape the trudge of his contemporaries and connect with the wellspring of art: the raw excitement of rejuvenating 'barbarism'. Had he wished, the Devil might have quoted any number of recent heretics – say, Gian Pietro Lucini ('For us, the Mystery lies within, / Inside the boundless shudder / That pulls, judges, and rejects, / The exalted frenzy / Of all the senses').

Leverkühn is cheated of the artistic reward he has hoped for. Although he completes his ambitious work – *Apocalypse* – the piece lacks the spirituality of the biblical text on which it is based. By Zeitblom's account, the image of the world's end that the composer conjures up is not sublime so much as terrifying, like a 'shapeless . . . germ of tentacles' in sound.[44] By seeking 'mystical passion' beyond the constricted 'bourgeois' realm he has renounced, Leverkühn drags the rarefied aesthetic sphere down into the bowels of the earth. The noble savagery promised by unhinged 'vital efficacy' amounts to noise; unclean hands are unfit to touch Holy Writ.

Deprived of the cleansing musical fire he had envisioned, Leverkühn presses on after *Apocalypse* and sets about working on *The Lamentation of Doctor Faustus*, the whimper after the bang. Slowly but surely, he succumbs to crippling disease and wasting sorrow. When he finishes the score, he is only a husk of his former self; instead of sharing the music with his friends, he recounts the tale of his infernal contract and lapses into delirium that lasts until death.

Leverkühn's life and times – as recounted by a less astute contemporary, whose slight cluelessness forms part of the story, too – are to be taken in the framework of universal human beggary. Zeitblom scratches his head for what seems like eternity, but his exceptional friend, on a creaturely level, has the same

Liberated into atrocity: Lucas Cranach the Elder, *The Werewolf; or, The Cannibal*, 1510–15, woodcut print.

failings as everyone else. When given the chance, Leverkühn pursues what he wants, as blindly as any other mortal. Talent does not amount to grandeur. It doesn't even make for good art.

Hard of Hearing

We cannot hear *The Lamentation of Doctor Faustus*, only read the description Zeitblom offers of his own alienated response. Mann makes his narrator a little too pedantic to appreciate exactly how the mad composer's work relates to world events. The author didn't have a full view either. The classical tonality and instrumentation that 'Faustus' dismantles in the fiction fell apart in historical reality, too – and with them, the schemes for understanding the times. Zeitblom is left hanging between twelve-tone flights and marching jackboots, uncomprehending and distraught.

Mann's fellow exile from Hitler's Germany, Theodor Adorno, shared the novelist's dismay at, and distaste for, the course Western civilization had followed. In particular, he despised mass culture. National Socialism had made the danger of 'groupthink' plain.

Yet Germany was hardly the only land where uniformization threatened to level the spiritual dimension that makes human life meaningful. In a 1941 essay, Adorno diagnosed what he witnessed in the United States as pathological.

The whole structure of popular music is standardized, even where the attempt is made to circumvent standardization. Standardization extends from the most general features to the most specific ones. Best known is the rule that the chorus consists of thirty-two bars and that the range is limited to one octave and one note. The general types of hits are also standardized . . . The harmonic cornerstones of each hit . . . beat out the standard scheme. This scheme emphasizes the most primitive harmonic facts no matter what has harmonically intervened . . . This inexorable device guarantees that regardless of what aberrations occur, the hit will lead back to the same familiar experience, and nothing fundamentally novel will be introduced.[45]

Predictably sugarcoated harmonies and sentimental lyrics resemble nothing so much as automobiles, munitions or whatever else the 'culture industry' churns out. Just as junk food stills hunger but offers little nutritional value, canned culture may satiate the appetite, but it does not feed the soul and is stupid and sick. Inasmuch as 'nothing . . . novel is introduced', the promise of modernity itself, which is all about the *new* and *better*, is betrayed.

More a Leverkühn than a Zeitblom, Adorno championed difficult music: its dissonance and thorny edges demand attention and engagement; chords that remain unresolved, notes climbing and descending on unconventional scales and time signatures that do not lend themselves to toe-tapping open space for intellectual sparks to fly. If fissures and gaps in the realm of art prove unsettling, it means that the work has captured something of the tension pervading the social body and historical process. 'Serious music' is satanic in the biblical sense: it makes trial of listeners. It is not there to be consumed but to pose a challenge. Music that displeases vulgar ears spurs the mind and sharpens discernment, introducing room for reflection, the thinker's cardinal virtue.

Alas, time, technology and economic calculation have favoured the tastes of commoners and crowds. From their ranks, stomping 4/4 rhythms, blunt lyrical themes and youthful energy have filled, in successive waves, AM radio, FM broadcasting, music television and now the global advertising space of the Internet. Hereby, conformity has donned the mask of rebellion. Its soundtrack is rock 'n' roll, the swan song of the Faustian age.[46]

Rock 'n' roll is nothing if not primitive. Its grunts and howls signify that the modern world cannot escape its origin and destiny: the delight and doom of the Garden of Eden. *Venter* takes precedence over *caput*; guts, not brains, command the organism. Religious fundamentalists who have called this racket 'the Devil's music' mean that it celebrates lust, illusion and impatience over abiding truths. Marxian musicological mandarins think so, too.

Entertainers know as much, but they embrace their part in the undignified proceedings. At the height of their slouching powers, the Rolling Stones released 'Sympathy for the Devil' (1968). Grooving along in a beatified haze, the song passes history in review: the Devil oversees Pontius Pilate's judgement of Jesus, gleefully watches the early modern wars of religion, is there when the czar and his court are killed in twentieth-century Russia, and plays the part of a German general during the Second World War. The most recent event is the assassinations of the Kennedys. Midway through the song, a sparse chant comes in: 'woo woo', which also sounds like 'who who?' The message is that no one is innocent. Léon Bloy would have relished performing an exegesis of this commonplace.

Seasons of sport and folly are fated to pass. For decades now, radio – itself an archaic medium – has been broadcasting 'classic rock', a term that indicates the party is already over. Popular auto-tuned confections even more insipid than the last dozen records by Mick Jagger and his geriatric bandmates now pulse through the World Wide Web, which promises freedom and fulfilment through unlimited consumer choice but delivers pornography, punditry, spam and scams. 'Content' is at best a secondary consideration for digital profiteers. With a signal-to-noise ratio like that, only events heralding the Apocalypse have a chance of being

An uncanny ability to capture a likeness: Maarten van Heemskerck, *The Devil Fills the Human Heart with Lust for Riches, Power and Pleasure*, 1548–50, pen and ink on paper.

heard in the first place. So far, reports have amounted to bluffs and games in virtual reality. But the tweets, chat rooms and other forms of computerized promiscuity will fall silent yet. Individual and communal life has become a matter of getting a regular charge both literally (through a socket) and metaphorically (from up-to-the-minute news, limited-time-only offers, online petitions and so on). *Someone* will pull the plug, and probably sooner than people think. The Bible says so.

Coda

On 11 September 2001 terrorists hijacked four planes and turned them into projectiles aimed at the World Trade Center in New York and the Pentagon in Washington, DC. Amid the grief and outrage, the German composer Karlheinz Stockhausen shocked pious sensibilities when he likened the event to 'the greatest work of art that is possible in the whole cosmos'.[1] The remark received far more notice than anything an avant-garde artist usually says. Stockhausen hastened to clarify what he had meant: musicians 'practice like crazy, totally fanatically . . . and then die'. The terrorists had done the same, but to much greater effect. 'I couldn't do that. In comparison with that, we're nothing as composers.' Artistic efforts pale in comparison to such a 'satanic composition', which illustrates the might of 'Lucifer' to 'destroy creation'.

Perhaps without realizing as much, Stockhausen had played the Devil's advocate: making the case, against common opinion, for seeing a seemingly self-evident matter in a new light. In fact, his statements fell in line with what he had been doing for decades. The avant-garde embraces experimentation – trial and error – and seeks to provoke a different view of the world. Throughout a long and otherwise celebrated career, Stockhausen had tested standing notions of art, life and the relationship between them through non-standard intervals and surprising forms of instrumentation (the most relevant example being a string quartet and a helicopter).

Stockhausen is hardly alone in acknowledging the proximity between creation and destruction, or the fact that works of imagination may hold undesirable effects. Long, long ago, Plato declared that poets should be banished from the ideal state. More recently, Adorno contended that 'every work of art is an uncommitted crime.'[2] The idea has a real philosophical pedigree – and a theological one, too: biblical prohibitions on representation are quite plain. It is also telling that the attack on the financial centre made a greater impact, in symbolic terms, than the simultaneous strike on the headquarters of U.S. military operations. Media coverage glossed over the parallels between money and arms, as if the Twin Towers did not 'reach unto heaven' like giant missile silos before being 'scattered abroad upon the face of the whole earth' (Genesis 11:4).

Stockhausen was not endorsing the terrorists' actions. He was affirming an insight too readily forgotten in an age that considers aesthetics only in terms of diversion and personal taste. In fact, art is serious business – like finance, politics and warfare. The high-minded composer became the fall guy for an indignant society that was denied the possibility of making those directly responsible for the attacks answer for their deeds. They had died executing their designs. Not long afterward, the United States launched the so-called War on Terror, which did not counterbalance the destruction so much as widen its scope across the globe.

With passages of relative calm and angry swells, the infernal music continues. A philosopher might see the Hegelian dialectic at work:

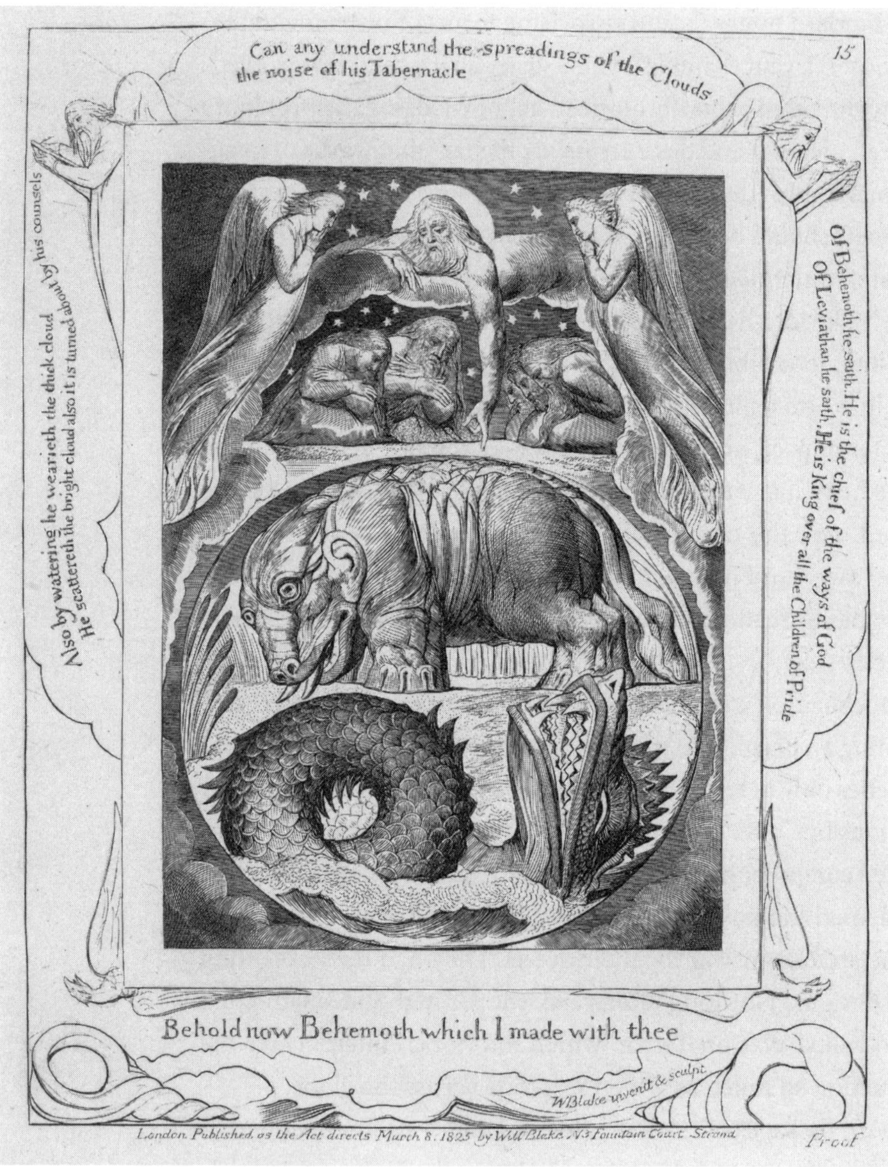

Creation, creator, and creatures: William Blake, 'Behemoth and Leviathan', from the series *The Book of Job*, 1825, line engraving on India paper.

We need only compile an accurate account of the misfortunes which have overtaken the finest manifestations of national and political life, and of personal virtues or innocence, to see a most terrifying picture take shape before our eyes. Its effect is to intensify our feelings to an extreme pitch of hopeless sorrow with no redeeming circumstances to counterbalance it. We can only harden ourselves against it or escape from it by telling ourselves that it was ordained by fate and could not have been otherwise . . . As we look upon history as an altar upon which the happiness of nations, the wisdom of states, and the virtue of individuals are slaughtered, our thoughts inevitably impel us to ask: to whom, or to what ultimate end have these monstrous sacrifices been made?[3]

Simpler minds would put the question in less high-flown language and respond in straightforward terms. The shorthand version sounds less like German Idealism or serial composition than the loudest and most belligerent form of rock music. On 9/11 thrash metal group Slayer released their ninth studio album: *God Hates Us All.*

With the exception of the occasional idiot,[4] no one who sets out to kill large numbers of people ever claims to be doing so for the sake of serving Satan. Poets and musicians might pretend otherwise, but they substitute symbolic gestures for real ones. Cults such as Anton LaVey's Church of Satan, which was founded in 1960s California and appealed to numerous entertainers (including Mick Jagger and, improbably enough, Sammy Davis Jr), follow a script that has been around since the Middle Ages, indulging in the clownishness of carnival season.[5] Supposedly transgressive bands, with their blasphemous chants and wild antics on- and offstage, are also buffoons. Even for the chronically immature, adolescence cannot last forever. Look online for the opinions of hard rockers such as Dave Mustaine (Megadeth) or James Hetfield (Metallica); they match those of other bloated middle-aged conservatives.

In fact, perpetrators of outrage, whether entrepreneurial or state-sponsored, appeal to the Lord when they kill. The terrorist strikes were performed by Muslim fundamentalists. The U.S. military response originally bore a title any Sunday school teacher would have advised against: 'Operation Infinite Justice'. The name sounds like a joke – Revelation for comic-book readers who want an action hero wearing a cape and brandishing a cross that shoots lasers. The attack and the counterattack formed two sides of the same cheap currency of profanation and presumption.

History remains an altar of human sacrifice performed by human beings. Both the Old and the New Testaments warn that an 'uncircumcised heart' is all it takes to make impious offerings that stink to divine nostrils. A little too late to benefit the Christians he persecuted before his conversion, the erstwhile Saul of Tarsus, St Paul, recognized that God alone can decide when violence is appropriate. 'Dearly beloved, avenge not yourselves, but rather give place unto wrath . . . "Vengeance is mine; I will repay," saith the Lord' (Romans 12:19). Providence will take care of settling scores.

If there can only be one God (or, by theological maths, three adumbrated versions of the Deity), there cannot be two. Satan has no right to use force at will. He must follow orders and play second fiddle eternally. His unique purpose authenticated by Scripture is to test and try belief, and especially the faith of the righteous. Everything else represents a later gloss or, more commonly, a fabrication.

The Devil as a cosmic force working to his own ends is mythology, pure and simple, no matter how influential or commanding the idea has proven. And even if he plays the part of 'bad cop', Satan has never *caused* anything. At most, he has helped those already inclined to wickedness accomplish ignoble aims – in order to assure the damnation they merit. Anyone beset by trouble who would blame the Devil is looking for an easy way out. Human beings are always at fault.

Nothing has changed since ancient times. Job asks: 'What? shall we receive good at the hand of God, and shall we not receive evil?' This rhetorical question may not offer as much comfort as we wish, but it contains wisdom. Job's wife proposes another answer to the woes of existence, but it offers no hope at all. 'Curse God', she tells her spouse, 'and die.'

REFERENCES

Introduction: Thank God for the Devil!

1 Daniel Defoe, *The Political History of the Devil* (London, 1726), p. 2.
2 Ibid.
3 Ibid., pp. 3, 4.
4 William D. Crano, *The Rules of Influence: Winning When You're in the Minority* (New York, 2012), pp. 20–21.

1 The Case for the Prosecution

1 While dated and very much the product of its day, the King James translation represents a standard of eloquence in the English language. Because of its pathos and resonance, it is used here, with commentary when a more literal translation brings out relevant aspects of the original. For the history and politics behind this epoch-making endeavour, see Adam Nicolson, *God's Secretaries: The Making of the King James Bible* (New York, 2005).
2 Neil Forsyth, *The Old Enemy: Satan and the Combat Myth* (Princeton, NJ, 1987), pp. 114–15.
3 Robert Alter, *The Wisdom Books: Job, Proverbs, and Ecclesiastes: A Translation with Commentary* (New York, 2011), p. 13.
4 See René Girard, *Job: The Victim of His People*, trans. Yvonne Freccero (Baltimore, MD, 1987).
5 The first to speak is Eliphaz the Temanite: 'Remember, I pray thee, who ever perished, being innocent? Or where were the righteous cut off? Even as I have seen, they that plow iniquity, and sow wickedness, reap the same. By the blast of God they perish, and by the breath of his nostrils are they consumed' (4:7–9).

6 Robert Alter points out that while Job speaks in 'vividly powerful language', the text reserves 'still greater poetry for God': 'The wide-ranging panorama of creation in the Voice from the Whirlwind shows . . . sublimity of expression . . . plasticity of description, [and] an ability to evoke the complex and dynamic interplay of beauty and violence in the natural world . . . God's thundering challenge to Job is not bullying. Rather, it . . . introduces a comprehensive overview of the nature of reality' (Alter, *Wisdom Books*, p. 10). See Alter's own translation.

7 See the materials gathered in Victor H. Matthews and Don C. Benjamin, *Old Testament Parallels: Laws and Stories from the Ancient Near East* (Mahwah, NJ, 2006).

8 For example, Isaiah: 'Hear, O heavens, and give ear, O earth: for the Lord hath spoken, "I have nourished and brought up children, and they have rebelled against me. The ox knoweth his owner, and the ass his master's crib: but Israel doth not know, my people doth not consider." Ah sinful nation, a people laden with iniquity, a seed of evildoers, children that are corrupters: they have forsaken the Lord, they have provoked the Holy One of Israel unto anger, they are gone away backward. Why should ye be stricken any more? Ye will revolt more and more: the whole head is sick, and the whole heart faint. From the sole of the foot even unto the head there is no soundness in it; but wounds, and bruises, and putrefying sores' (2–6).

9 Forsyth, *The Old Enemy*, pp. 21–89.

10 Elaine Pagels, *The Origin of Satan: How Christians Demonized Jews, Pagans, and Heretics* (New York, 1996), p. 47.

11 Ibid.; see T. J. Wray and Gregory Mobley, *The Birth of Satan: Tracing the Devil's Biblical Roots* (New York, 2005), pp. 107–8.

12 Pagels, *The Origin of Satan*, pp. 57ff.

13 See James H. Charlesworth, *The Good and Evil Serpent: How a Universal Symbol Became Christianized* (New Haven, CT, 2010), pp. 269–351.

14 See Jean-Pierre Vernant, *Myth and Society in Ancient Greece*, trans. Janet Lloyd (New York, 1988), pp. 183–202.

15 See Wray and Mobley, *The Birth of Satan*, pp. 69–70.

16 That said, 'like most of the explanations of names in Genesis, this is probably based on folk etymology or an imaginative playing with sound . . . In the Hebrew . . . the phonetic similarity is between *ḥawah*, "Eve", and the verbal root *ḥayah*, "to live"'

(Robert Alter, *The Five Books of Moses: A Translation with Commentary* [New York, 2004], p. 27).

17 Forsyth, *The Old Enemy*, pp. 134–9.

18 On the genesis of these texts, see I. Gafni, 'The Historical Background', in Michael E. Stone, ed., *Jewish Writings of the Second Temple Period* (Philadelphia, PA, 1984), pp. 1–32.

19 For discussion of the many versions, see Loren Stuckenbruck, *The Myth of Rebellious Angels: Studies in Second Temple Judaism and New Testament Texts* (Grand Rapids, MI, 2014), as well as G.W.E. Nickelsburg, 'The Bible Rewritten and Expanded', in *Jewish Writings*, ed. Stone, pp. 89–117.

20 The story appeared in other iterations, too. Its scant support in the Tanakh comes from a tendentious reading of Ezekiel. See Wray and Mobley, *The Birth of Satan*, pp. 108–10.

21 Gabriele Boccaccini, *Roots of Rabbinic Judaism: An Intellectual History from Ezekiel to Daniel* (Grand Rapids, MI, 2002), pp. 89–103.

22 See the entry 'Nephilim', *Dictionary of Deities and Demons in the Bible*, pp. 618–20.

23 Pagels, *The Origin of Satan*, pp. 50–51.

24 Paula Friedriksen, *From Jesus to Christ: The Origins of the New Testament Images of Christ* (New Haven, CT, 2000).

25 Pagels, *The Origin of Satan*, pp. 80–81.

26 Ibid., p. 81.

27 Ibid.

28 Richard A. Horsley, *Bandits, Prophets, and Messiahs: Popular Movements at the Time of Jesus* (London, 1999).

29 Pagels, *The Origin of Satan*, p. 7.

30 Ibid., pp. 39–40.

31 From a rigorously Christian perspective, this statement does not hold: Jesus makes an offering of himself, thereby exposing the sacrificial mechanism underlying false religion; see René Girard, *Things Hidden Since the Foundation of the World*, trans. Stephen Bann and Michael Metteer (Stanford, CA, 1987), especially pp. 180–223.

32 The ancient source for first-century events is *The Jewish War* by Flavius Josephus, who switched from the Jewish to the Roman side. For discussion of this fascinating turncoat and his times, see Mireille Hadas-Lebel, *Flavius Josephus: Eyewitness to Rome's First-century Conquest of Judea*, trans. Richard Miller (New

York, 1993). Martin Goodman, *Rome and Jerusalem: The Clash of Ancient Civilizations* (New York, 2008) provides an account of both the big picture and pivotal episodes.

33 Leonard W. Levy, *Treason Against God: A History of the Offense of Blasphemy* (New York, 1981), p. 33.

34 The only title Jesus claims for himself is 'Son of Man', which echoes the Book of Daniel (7:13). To call oneself in this way represents a bold gesture with messianic connotations, but such implications would have been unintelligible to pagan ears.

35 Levy, *Treason Against God*, p. 54.

36 Ibid., p. 61.

37 Relevant indictments from the Old Testament include Exodus 32:9 and 33:3–5; Deuteronomy 9:6 and 9:12–13; 2 Kings 17:13–14; and 2 Chronicles 36:15–16. The New Testament brings the charges to bear on the present generation (for example, Acts 7:51: 'Ye stiffnecked and uncircumcised in heart and ears, ye do always resist the Holy Ghost: as your fathers did, so do ye.')

38 See Matthew 5:17.

2 Satan and Salvation

1 For an overview of the cultural and political circumstances of his day and informed conjecture about his purposes, see Elaine Pagels, *Revelations: Visions, Prophecy, and Politics in the Book of Revelation* (New York, 2012), especially pp. 7–13, 16, 30–35.

2 See John J. Collins, *The Apocalyptic Imagination: An Introduction to Jewish Apocalyptic Literature* (Grand Rapids, MI, 1998), pp. 1–42; Stephen D. O'Leary, *Arguing the Apocalypse: A Theory of Millennial Rhetoric* (Oxford, 1998), pp. 3–19.

3 On echoes of earlier prophets, in particular Daniel, see Pagels, *Revelations*, pp. 30–32.

4 See Pagels, *Revelations*, pp. 96–7; Richard Bauckham, *The Theology of the Book of Revelation* (Cambridge, 1993), pp. 66–108.

5 Pagels, *The Origin of Satan*, p. 49.

6 Henry Ansgar Kelly, *Satan: A Biography* (Cambridge, 2006), p. 159.

7 Ibid., p. 155.

8 See Pagels, *Revelations*, pp. 46–7.

9 Christian readers have long taken these words as an indictment of those who reject Jesus. However, such an interpretation is anachronistic. John was addressing an audience that adhered to

ancestral ways. Those who wrongly claimed to be Jews, in his eyes, were Gentile converts to a compromised form of Judaism – parties who embraced Jesus but did not observe dietary prohibitions, practice circumcision and so on. See Pagels, *Revelations*, pp. 59–60.

10 Pagels, *Revelations*, pp. 32–3.

11 See Kelly Olson, *Masculinity and Dress in Roman Antiquity* (London, 2017), pp. 49–50, 109–16.

12 Pagels, *The Origin of Satan*, p. xii.

13 See David Potter, *Constantine the Emperor* (Oxford, 2013), pp. 150–59.

14 Peter Brown, *The Rise of Western Christendom: Triumph and Diversity, AD 200–1000* (Oxford, 1997) is a standard work; for a much less charitable assessment, see Catherine Nixey, *The Darkening Age: The Christian Destruction of the Classical World* (New York, 2018).

15 T. R. Glover and Gerald H. Rendall, trans., *Tertullian: Apology, De Spectaculis. Minucius Felix: Octavius* (Cambridge, MA, 1931), p. 337; the passage quoted below comes from the same and following pages (chapter IX).

16 Brown, *The Body and Society*, p. 120.

17 Ibid., p. 69.

18 'Civilization', Freud writes, 'favours every path by which strong identifications can be established between the members of the community, and it summons up aim-inhibited libido on the largest scale' (Sigmund Freud, *Civilization and Its Discontents*, trans. James Strachey [New York, 1989], p. 99). See p. 108 for his remarks on Christianity and Roman religion.

19 Brown, *The Body and Society*, p. 132.

20 In a comparative analysis of Christian and pagan conceptions of sexuality, Michel Foucault draws attention to the problem of 'extreme asceticism that does not take the form of observance of the law, but whose function and meaning is . . . to go beyond the domain of the law' – in other words, 'antinomianism' (Michel Foucault, *On the Government of the Living: Lectures at the Collège de France, 1979–1980*, trans. Graham Burchell [New York, 2016], p. 184).

21 John Scheid, *An Introduction to Roman Religion*, trans. Janet Lloyd (Bloomington, IN, 2003), pp. 129–46, aptly speaks of 'priestly figures' in all spheres of Roman life.

22 See the next chapter.
23 Pagels, *Revelations*, especially pp. 133–70.

3 The Adversary at Home and Abroad

1 This does not mean that such a notion did not exist. *Sheol* ('pit' or 'grave') is the Hebrew name for where the dead 'live'. Jeffrey Burton Russell writes: 'The Jewish idea of reward in another world goes back at least to the seventh century BCE, and the distinction between faithful and unfaithful Jews increased in the sixth century during the Babylonian Captivity, when much of the Hebrew Bible was written down. The suffering of the people of Israel during the Captivity helped shift the focus of Jewish hope from blessedness on earth to blessedness in the other life. The separation between the good and the evil dead produced modifications in the idea of Sheol. Part of Sheol was identified with Gehenna, the valley near Jerusalem where rubbish was dumped and continuously burned . . . Another part of Sheol remained the shadowy abode of the mediocre. A third part, reserved for the qehel [i.e., *qehel Adonai*, "Lord's remnant"] became a place of rest and comfort' (*A History of Heaven: The Singing Silence* (Princeton, NJ, 1999), pp. 27–28). A more nuanced vision developed during the Second Temple Period (*c.* 500 BCE – 70 CE). In turn, the biblical prophets' visions of punishment and reward provided the basis for ideas about the order of 'the world to come' recorded in the Talmud.
2 For an overview of sources and influential commentary, see Erwin Rohde, *Psyche: The Cult of Souls and the Belief in Immortality among the Greeks*, trans. W. B. Hillis (London, 1925).
3 See the classic work (1864) by Numa Denis Fustel de Coulanges, *The Ancient City: A Study on the Religion, Laws, and Institutions of Greece and Rome*, trans. Willard Small (Baltimore, MD, 1980), especially pp. 17–25.
4 In the words of an incredulous Greek observer from the fourth century BCE, 'The Egyptians regard the time spent in this life as completely worthless . . . Indeed, they refer to the houses of the living as "inns" . . . , since we dwell in them but a short time, while the tombs of the dead they call "everlasting homes"' (quoted in Jan Assmann, *Death and Salvation in Ancient Egypt*, trans. David Lorton (Ithaca, NY, 2005), p. 375).

5 Tim Whitmarsh, *Battling the Gods: Atheism in the Ancient World* (New York, 2015).

6 George E. Mylonas, *Eleusis and the Eleusinian Mysteries* (Princeton, NJ, 1961) presents a thorough account from an archeological perspective.

7 See Manfred Clauss, *The Roman Cult of Mithras: The God and His Mysteries*, trans. Richard Gordon (London, 2001), who stresses that the Roman deity Mithras should not be directly equated with Mitra in Iran.

8 Walter Burkert, *Ancient Mystery Cults* (Cambridge, MA, 1987), offers a critical assessment of scholarly commonplaces and opts for 'a decidedly pagan approach': 'Initiation at Eleusis or worship of Isis or Mithras does not constitute adherence to a religion in the sense we are familiar with, being confronted with mutually exclusive religions such as Judaism, Christianity, and Islam . . . In the pre-Christian epoch the various forms of worship . . . are never exclusive; they appear as varying forms, trends, or options within the one disparate yet continuous conglomerate of ancient religion' (pp. 3–4).

9 See Chapter Seven.

10 See Martin Goodman, *Judaism in the Roman World: Collected Essays* (Leiden, 2007), pp. 91–116.

11 'The Lord hath prepared his throne in the heavens, and his kingdom ruleth over all' (Psalm 103:19).

12 Jacques Le Goff, *The Birth of Purgatory*, trans. Arthur Goldhammer (Chicago, IL, 1986), pp. 52–3.

13 Ibid., p. 66.

14 Augustine, *Confessions*, trans. Henry Chadwick (Oxford, 2009), p. 123.

15 Quotations are by canto and line number; with occasional modification, they follow Dante Alighieri, *The Divine Comedy: Inferno, Purgatorio, Paradiso*, trans. Allen Mandelbaum (New York, 1995).

16 As is the case for Fra Alberigo and Branca Doria, in Canto XXXIII.

17 Dante, *Inferno*, I, 70–75.

18 Ibid., XXXIV, 30–31.

19 Ibid., XXXIV, 6.

20 Ibid., XXXIV, 38–54.

21 Indeed, the pilgrim meets him in Canto X of *Paradiso*.

22 Paul J. Glenn, *A Tour of the Summa* (London, 1963), p. 94.

23 Dante, *Inferno*, XXVII, 123.

24 See Richard Lansing, ed., *The Dante Encyclopedia* (London, 2010), pp. 362–5.

25 See *Inferno*, VII, 47, where many 'clergymen, and popes and cardinals' appear in the Fourth Circle (Greed). Canto XIX features one pope, Nicholas III, who announces the imminent arrival of his successor, Boniface VIII, and, in due course, that of their mutual heir, Clement V.

26 Robert Muchembled, *A History of the Devil: From the Middle Ages to the Present*, trans. Jean Birrell (Oxford, 2003), p. 27.

27 Dante, *Inferno*, XXXIV, 28.

28 Ibid., III, 84–5.

29 Ibid., XVII.

30 Consider John Ruskin's appreciation: 'Wherever the human mind is healthy and vigorous in all its proportions, great in imagination and emotion no less than in intellect . . . there the grotesque will exist in full energy. And accordingly, I believe that there is no test of greatness in periods, nations, or men, more sure than the development . . . of a noble grotesque . . . I think that the central man of all the world, as representing in perfect balance the imaginative, moral, and intellectual faculties, is Dante' (*The Genius of John Ruskin: Selections from His Writings*, ed. John D. Rosenberg [Charlottesville, VA, 1998], p. 214.

31 Historian Clifford R. Backman writes: 'The question of literacy in the Middle Ages is a difficult one to answer since there is no clear way of studying it. The mere existence of written materials from any time period, even the vastly increased existence of them hardly proves anything . . . Medieval people are frequently described in legal documents as being either *literatus* or *illiteratus*, and *sciens* or *idiota* (meaning "literate", "illiterate", "knowledgeable", and "uneducated", respectively) – but it is unclear whether these terms refer to the ability to read, the ability to read *and* write, the ability to read and/or write *in Latin* as well as the vernacular, or the ability to read and/or write *in only the vernacular*. Sometimes the documents appear to describe the ability to *speak* Latin without suggesting anything at all about the ability to read it or write it. At other times the terms appear to describe the extent of a person's

formal education' (*The Worlds of Medieval Europe* (Oxford, 2003), p. 345).

32 Jeffrey Burton Russell, *Lucifer: The Devil in the Middle Ages* (Ithaca, NY, 1984), p. 63; the next quote comes from the same page.

33 E. K. Chambers, *The Mediaeval Stage*, 2 vols (Oxford, 1903), vol. I, p. 94.

34 Georges Duby, *The Age of the Cathedrals: Art and Society, 980–1420*, trans. Eleanor Levieux and Barbara Thompson (Chicago, IL, 1983).

35 Russell, *Lucifer*, p. 63.

36 Quotations below follow the text printed in *The Riverside Chaucer*, ed. Larry D. Benson (Boston, 1987), pp. 3–328, by fragment group and line number.

37 Chaucer, *Canterbury Tales*, III, 1392–4.

38 Ibid., III, 1448.

39 Ibid., III, 1674.

40 Ibid., III, 1689.

41 Ibid., III, 1868.

42 Ibid., I, 624.

43 Mikhail Bakhtin, *Problems of Dostoevsky's Poetics*, trans. Caryl Emerson (Minneapolis, MN, 1984), pp. 129–30.

44 Chambers, *Mediaeval Stage*, II, p. 3. See John D. Cox, *The Devil and the Sacred in English Drama, 1350–1642* (Cambridge, 2000) for an important critique of his predecessor's methodology in general and his analysis of stage devils in particular. 'In E. K. Chambers' view, vernacular drama's recognition of secular problems was impossible for liturgical drama, because it was preoccupied with spiritual and otherworldly concerns. He therefore understood occasional moments of social satire in the mystery plays, often voiced through devils, as evidence of secularity and evolutionary progress. He was right about a sense of opposition in early drama . . . but the opposition did not involve secular and sacred; rather, it involved God and the devil' (p. 19). Cox's objection to 'a narrative of teleological secularization' (p. 1) is well-taken.

45 Chambers, *Mediaeval Stage*, vol. II, p. 77.

46 Ibid., pp. 2–3.

4 Doubt, Dissent and the Devil

1 Diarmaid MacCulloch, *Christianity: The First Three Thousand Years* (New York, 2009) offers a remarkably thorough and even-handed account; see pp. 112–228 for early doctrinal disputes.

2 Robert Burton, *The Anatomy of Melancholy* (New York, 2001), p. 196.

3 *Hamlet*, II.ii.599–600; quoted from *The Riverside Shakespeare* (Boston, 1974).

4 Diarmaid MacCulloch, *Reformation: Europe's House Divided, 1490–1700* (London, 2004), p. 123.

5 Ibid., p. 110.

6 Ibid.

7 Ibid., p. 107.

8 Ibid., p. 114.

9 Quoted in Roland Herbert Bainton, *Here I Stand: A Life of Martin Luther* (New York, 1950), p. 127.

10 Ibid., p. 139.

11 Ibid., p. 134; see p. 147.

12 See Pagels, *Revelations*, p. 173: 'Lutherans published Lucas Cranach's pictures of the pope as the whore of Babylon in one of the first Lutheran Bibles, while an early Catholic biographer retaliated by depicting Luther, on the frontispiece, as the seven-headed beast.'

13 MacCulloch, *Reformation*, p. 123.

14 For a good overview, see C. Scott Dixon, *The Reformation in Germany* (Oxford, 2002).

15 In his 1522 'Preface to the Revelation of St. John', Luther had declared: 'I will leave this book . . . to each one's opinion and will bind no one to my thoughts or estimation of it . . . This book leaves so much to be desired that I hold it to be neither apostolic nor prophetic. In the first place, the apostles do not use visions, but prophesy with plain, clear words, as Peter, Paul, and Christ do in the gospel . . . Besides, there is no prophet in the Old Testament, not to mention the New, who so uses visions and images throughout . . . I cannot tell that it is inspired by the Holy Spirit' (Philip D. W. Krey and Peter D. S. Krey, trans., *Luther's Spirituality* [New York, 2007], p. 47).

16 Relevant documents are found in Michael G. Baylor, ed., *The Radical Reformation* (Cambridge, 1991). Norman Cohn,

The Pursuit of the Millennium: Revolutionary Millenarians and Mystical Anarchists of the Middle Ages (Oxford, 1970), provides a genealogy and context for events.

17 C. V. Wedgwood, *The Thirty Years War* (New York, 1984), p. 511. For a more recent assessment, see Geoffrey Parker, *The Thirty Years' War* (London, 1997), pp. 186–202.

18 See Chapter One.

19 For a concise account, see Robert J. Knecht, *The French Religious Wars, 1562–1598* (Oxford, 2002).

20 Théodore Agrippa d'Aubigné, *Oeuvres complètes*, 6 vols (Paris, 1877), vol. IV, p. 240; here and elsewhere, translations not otherwise credited are my own.

21 For an account that stresses the monarch's political shrewdness – and ruthlessness – see G. W. Bernard, *The King's Reformation: Henry VIII and the Remaking of the English Church* (New Haven, CT, 2005).

22 Thomas Cranmer, *Miscellaneous Writings and Letters* (Cambridge, 1846), p. 64.

23 Ibid., p. 62.

24 Lewis W. Spitz, *The Protestant Reformation: 1517–1559* (New York, 1985), pp. 101–28, does an especially good job discussing the social-historical and economic aspects of events.

25 MacCulloch, *Reformation*, pp. 237–47. Describing the general trend, Spitz writes: 'The Reformation was in part a defeudalization of the church in which the urban centers asserted their rights against the prince-bishops . . . The city replaced the monastery as the center for literary culture; the city chronicles supplanted the monastic chronicles and annals . . . Religious reform necessarily involved social reform, for with the emphasis on the priesthood of all believers the medieval distinction of clergy and laity disappeared' (*Protestant Reformation*, pp. 183–4).

26 MacCulloch, *Reformation*, pp. 198–204.

27 See the classic study by Elizabeth L. Eisenstein, *The Printing Press as an Agent of Change* (Cambridge, 1979).

28 See Philip Mason Palmer and Robert Pattison More, *The Sources of the Faust Tradition: From Simon Magus to Lessing* (Oxford, 1936).

29 Ian Watt, *Myths of Modern Individualism: Faust, Don Quixote, Don Juan, Robinson Crusoe* (Cambridge, 1997).

30 August Kühne, ed., *Das älteste Faustbuch: Wortgetreuer Abdruck der editio princeps des Spies'schen Faustbuches vom Jahre 1587* (Zerbst, 1868); the next quote is taken from p. 134.

31 Watt, *Myths of Modern Individualism*, p. 32.

32 A valuable guide to the author's life and works is Patrick Cheney, ed., *The Cambridge Companion to Christopher Marlowe* (Cambridge, 2004); see, in particular, the contributions by Paul Whitefield White, 'Marlowe and the Politics of Religion', pp. 70–89, and Thomas Healy, 'Doctor Faustus', pp. 174–92.

33 In the words of a disapproving contemporary; quoted in Tom Rutter, *The Cambridge Introduction to Christopher Marlowe* (Cambridge, 2012), p. 122.

34 Park Honan, *Christopher Marlowe: Poet and Spy* (Oxford, 2006), sifts through all the facts and conjecture to offer a gripping account of the author's life.

35 There are two versions of the play (both of which appeared after the author's death). References indicate the scene and line number of the earlier 'A text' (1604), as printed in Christopher Marlowe, *The Works of Christopher Marlowe*, ed. A. H. Bullen, 3 vols (London, 1884), vol. I, pp. 207–83. Here: Prologue, 20–24 ('Till, swoll'n with cunning of a self-conceit / His waxen wings did mount above his reach, And melting heavens conspired his overthrow').

36 Marlowe, *Tragical History of Doctor Faustus*, XVI, 126–30.

37 Ibid., V, 11.

38 Ibid., I, 80–95.

39 Ibid., XIV, 45.

40 Ibid., XV, 103–4; the block quote below follows directly (106–11).

41 See Chapter Three.

42 H. R. Trevor-Roper, *The European Witch-craze of the Sixteenth and Seventeenth Centuries, and Other Essays* (New York, 1969).

43 See Jeffrey Burton Russell, *Witchcraft in the Middle Ages* (Ithaca, NY, 1984), pp. 63–100.

44 The term is a misnomer inasmuch as there was never a centralized inquisition, but only site-specific operations (for example, the Spanish Inquisition of the fifteenth century). See Edward Peters, *Inquisition* (Berkeley, CA, 1989), especially pp. 122–54.

45 R. I. Moore, *The War on Heresy* (Cambridge, MA, 2014), has
   argued that there was no unified opposition to Catholicism, if
   not within the evolving Church itself; most of what has entered
   historical record about this and other persecuted groups is a myth
   or, at very least, clerical projection after the fact.
46 Norman Cohn, *Europe's Inner Demons: An Enquiry Inspired
   by the Great Witch-hunt* (New York, 1975), p. 225.
47 MacCulloch, *Christianity*, p. 143.
48 Quoted in Pagels, *Revelations*, pp. 114–15.
49 See Joshua Trachtenberg, *The Devil and the Jews: The Medieval
   Conception of the Jew and Its Relation to Modern Anti-Semitism*
   (Lincoln, NE, 2002).
50 See Robert Chazan, *European Jewry and the First Crusade*
   (Berkeley, CA, 1987), pp. 27–37.
51 Cohn, *Europe's Inner Demons*, p. 237.
52 Methods used to obtain bodily 'proof', in turn, represent one
   of the most scandalous aspects of trials; see Walter Stephens,
   Demon Lovers: Witchcraft, Sex, and the Crisis of Belief (Chicago,
   IL, 2003), for a discussion of corporeality in early modern
   conceptions of witchcraft and forensic procedure.
53 Cohn, *Europe's Inner Demons*, p. 239.
54 Ibid., p. 232.
55 Ibid., pp. 252–3.
56 Trevor-Roper speaks of the witch as 'the universal scapegoat
   of the Wars of Religion' (*The European Witch-craze*, p. 111).
57 'During the age of the Reformation, Europeans increased
   their awareness of the Devil's presence in the world . . . One
   of the main sources of this heightened consciousness of, and
   militancy against, diabolical power was the thinking of the
   great Protestant reformers . . . [Yet] their beliefs were essentially
   the same as those of late medieval Catholic demonologists
   . . . Since the reformers challenged so many other aspects
   of medieval Catholicism, and since they were so critical of
   scholastic theology, one assumes they would have developed a
   distinctly Protestant demonology. Instead they merely adopted
   the traditional, late medieval view, modifying it only in some
   respects and placing it on a firmer scriptural foundation' (Brian
   P. Levack, *The Witch-hunt in Early Modern Europe* (London,
   2006), p. 112).

5 The Devil's Party

1 See Carl Schmitt, *The Leviathan in the State Theory of Hobbes: Meaning and Failure of a Political Symbol*, trans. George Schwab and Erna Hilfstein (Chicago, IL, 2008).

2 For example, 'there is no such thing as perpetuall Tranquillity of mind, while we live here; because Life it selfe is but Motion, and can never be without Desire, nor without Feare, no more than without Sense. What kind of Felicity God hath ordained to them that devoutly honour him, a man shall no sooner know, than enjoy' (Thomas Hobbes, *Leviathan*, ed. C. B. Macpherson (New York, 1985), pp. 129–30 [part I, chapter 7]). See Alexandre Koyré, *From the Closed World to the Infinite Universe* (Baltimore, MD, 1957).

3 For discussion and details, see Barbara K. Lewalski, *The Life of John Milton: A Critical Biography* (Oxford, 2003).

4 With occasional modifications of orthography, quotations follow the text printed in John Milton, *Complete Poems and Major Prose*, ed. Merritt Y. Hughes (New York, 1957), pp. 207–469, by book and line number; here: *Paradise Lost*, I, 16, 25–6.

5 Ibid., I, 13, 6.

6 Ibid., I, 7.

7 See Chapter One.

8 William Blake, *The Complete Poetry and Prose of William Blake*, ed. David V. Erdman (Berkeley, CA, 1982), p. 35.

9 Milton, *Paradise Lost*, I, 81.

10 Ibid., I, 24.

11 Blake, *The Complete Poetry*, p. 35.

12 Milton, *Paradise Lost*, I, 27–33.

13 Ibid., I, 34.

14 Ibid., I, 45–7.

15 Ibid., I, 125.

16 Ibid., V, 787–96.

17 Ibid., I, 757 and 43.

18 Ibid., V, 763.

19 Ibid., V, 798–9.

20 Ibid., V, 776–7.

21 Ibid., I, 756.

22 Ibid., IV, 690–91; V, 129.

23 Ibid., II, 927–38.

24 Ibid., ii, 940–42, 949–50.

25 Ibid., iv, 800–809.

26 Ibid., iii, 99.

27 Ibid., x, 554.

28 Ibid., i, 263.

29 Johann Wolfgang von Goethe, *Faust*, trans. Walter Kaufmann (New York, 1990), p. 87 [ll. 296–7]; hereafter cited by line number.

30 Ibid., 299.

31 Ibid., 302, 312.

32 In part, it reads: 'I have, alas, studied philosophy, / Jurisprudence and medicine, too, / And, worst of all, theology / With keen endeavor, through and through – / And here I am, for all my lore, / The wretched fool I was before' (ibid., 354ff.)

33 Ibid., 430–39; translation modified.

34 Ibid., 454–5.

35 Ibid., 460–63.

36 Ibid., 693.

37 Jane K. Brown, *Goethe's Allegories of Identity* (Philadelphia, PA, 2014), p. 137.

38 Goethe, *Faust*, 1338.

39 Ibid., 1766–71.

40 Ibid., 2603.

41 Ibid., 3871–5.

42 Ibid., 3906–11.

43 Ibid., 4183–8.

44 Ibid., 4189–90.

45 Mephisto asks in derision: 'You would fly, but get dizzy?' Significantly, the scene is in prose (and hence without a line number [pp. 399–405 in the Kaufmann edition; p. 400 for the remark in question]).

46 Goethe, *Faust*, 322.

47 See Fiona MacCarthy, *Byron: Life and Legend* (New York, 2002).

48 Andrew Rutherford, ed., *Lord Byron: The Critical Heritage* (London, 1995), pp. 179–81.

49 Byron, *The Major Works*, ed. Jerome J. McGann (Oxford, 1986), p. 265.

50 Ibid., p. 266.

51 Reinhart Koselleck, *The Practice of Conceptual History: Timing History, Spacing Concepts*, trans. Todd Samuel Preisner et al. (Stanford, CA, 2002), pp. 5–6.

52 See Nicholas Boyle's excellent biography, *Goethe: The Poet and the Age*, 2 vols (Oxford, 2000).

53 Heinrich Heine, *The Romantic School and Other Essays*, ed. Jost Hermand and Robert C. Holub (New York, 2002), p. 223.

54 See Elizabeth M. Butler, *The Fortunes of Faust* (University Park, PA, 1998), pp. 305–8.

55 Heinrich Heine, *Poems and Ballads*, trans. Emma Lazarus (New York, 1881), p. 90.

56 See Priscilla P. Ferguson, *Paris as Revolution: Writing the Nineteenth-century City* (Berkeley, CA, 1994), pp. 59–64.

57 Charles Baudelaire, *My Heart Laid Bare and Other Prose Writings*, trans. Norman Cameron (London, 1950), pp. 21–72; although the poet uses the title to describe his contemporary Constantin Guys (1802–1892), it names an ideal he embraced in his own work, too.

58 For an intricate analysis of the poet's perverse 'dance' with censors and the courts (where his verse landed him, on charges of blasphemy and indecency), see William Olmsted, *The Censorship Effect: Baudelaire, Flaubert, and the Formation of French Modernism* (Oxford, 2016), especially pp. 76–100.

59 Charles Baudelaire, *The Flowers of Evil*, trans. James N. McGowan (Oxford, 2008), p. 6.

60 Ibid., p. 269.

61 Ibid., p. 221.

62 See Helena Rosenblatt, *The Lost History of Liberalism: From Ancient Rome to the Twenty-first Century* (Princeton, NJ, 2018), particularly pp. 88–128.

63 See, for example, Louis Chevalier, *Laboring Classes and Dangerous Classes in Paris During the First Half of the Nineteenth Century* (New York, 1973).

64 Arthur Rimbaud, *Collected Poems*, trans. Martin Sorrel (Oxford, 2001), p. 211.

65 Ibid., p. 213.

66 See Chapter Seven.

67 Rimbaud, *Collected Poems*, p. 215.

68 See Graham Robb, *Rimbaud: A Biography* (New York, 2001), pp. 81–95.

69 Rimbaud, *Collected Poems*, p. 219. Nor, ultimately, were these words merely rhetorical; see Charles Nicholl, *Somebody Else: Arthur Rimbaud in Africa, 1880–1891* (Chicago, IL, 1997).

70 Rimbaud, *Collected Poems*, p. 219.
71 Frantz Fanon, *The Wretched of the Earth*, trans. Richard Philcox (New York, 2004), p. 162.

6 Sick, Sick, Sick

1 Throughout his diverse oeuvre, Michel Foucault addresses the shift from a relatively fixed index of knowledge and power to a system based on observation and testing, which demands constant reworking to qualify as 'true'. See *The Birth of the Clinic: An Archaeology of Medical Perception*, trans. Alan Sheridan (New York, 1973) and *The History of Sexuality*, vol. I: *An Introduction*, trans. Robert Hurley (New York, 1978), pp. 140–45.
2 On the author's life, works and thought, see Michel Lécureur, *Jules Barbey d'Aurevilly: Le Sagittaire* (Paris, 2008).
3 Max Nordau, *Degeneration* (New York, 1895), p. 297; originally published in German, 1892.
4 'Hysteria and neurasthenia are much more frequent in France . . . and can be studied far more closely in this country than anywhere else . . . It is precisely in France that the craziest fashions in art and literature . . . arise' (Nordau, *Degeneration*, p. 43).
5 See Michael Stanislawski, *Zionism and the Fin de Siècle: From Nordau to Jabotinsky* (Berkeley, CA, 2001).
6 Jules Barbey d'Aurevilly, *Diaboliques: Six Tales of Decadence*, trans. Raymond N. MacKenzie (Minneapolis, MN, 2015), pp. 76–7.
7 On these figures and the relevant cultural background, see Russell C. Maulitz, *Morbid Appearances: The Anatomy of Pathology in the Early Nineteenth Century* (Cambridge, 1987).
8 Barbey d'Aurevilly, *Diaboliques*, p. 79.
9 'The man was slender and patrician in his black coat, buttoned up correctly in the manner of a cavalry officer; if he had been wearing the kind of costume Titian gives to his characters, he would have resembled one of the courtiers of the era of Henri III, with his haughty yet feminine air, his mustaches as pointed as a cat's whiskers . . . and to make the resemblance more complete, he wore his hair short, so that one could see the glitter of two dark blue sapphire earrings' (ibid., p. 79).
10 Ibid., p. 79.

11 Ibid., p. 76.
12 Ibid., p. 83.
13 Ibid., p. 85.
14 Ibid., p. 86.
15 Ibid.
16 Ibid., pp. 86–7.
17 Ibid., p. 91.
18 Ibid., p. 87.
19 Ibid., p. 77; translation slightly modified.
20 For a magisterial account of Marx's thought and relevant biographical and historical information, see Isaiah Berlin, *Karl Marx* (Princeton, NJ, 2013).
21 Karl Marx, *The German Ideology: Including Theses on Feuerbach and Introduction to the Critique of Political Economy* (New York, 1998), p. 571.
22 See Chapter Five.
23 See Paul Thomas, *Marxism and Scientific Socialism: From Engels to Althusser* (London, 2008).
24 A highly readable recent biography is François Angelier's *Bloy ou la fureur du Juste* (Paris, 2015).
25 See Roy Morris, Jr, *Ambrose Bierce: Alone in Bad Company* (Oxford, 1995); see Chapter Four.
26 Léon Bloy, *Exégèse des lieux communs* (Paris, 1902), pp. 43–5.
27 On this group, see Martin Hengel, *The Zealots: Investigations into the Jewish Freedom Movement in the Period from Herod 1 until 70 AD*, trans. David Smith (Edinburgh, 1989).
28 Léon Bloy, *Les Dernières Colonnes de l'Église* (Paris, 1903), p. 220.
29 Léon Bloy, *Disagreeable Tales*, trans. Erik Butler (Cambridge, MA, 2015), p. 2; Joris K. Huysmans, *Là-bas (Down There)*, trans. Keene Wallace (New York, 1972), p. 259.
30 'How many children did he disembowel after deflowering them? He himself did not know, so many were the rapes he had consummated and the murders he had committed. The texts of the times enumerate between seven and eight hundred, but the estimate is inaccurate and seems overconservative. Entire regions were devastated' (p. 157).
31 Ibid., p. 54.
32 Ibid., p. 238.
33 Ibid., p. 114; translation slightly modified.
34 Ibid.

35 'He studied at a seminary in Brittany, [but] he had scruples
   of conscience and considered himself unworthy to enter the
   priesthood' (p. 39).
36 Ibid., p. 40.
37 Ibid., p. 42.
38 Ibid., p. 246.
39 Ibid., p. 248.
40 Ibid., p. 138.
41 Ibid., p. 155; translation modified.
42 Ibid., p. 159.
43 Ibid., p. 160.
44 Ibid.
45 On the emergence of the term and the array of meanings
   attached to it, see David Weir, *Decadence and the Making of
   Modern Culture* (Amherst, MA, 1995).
46 See Philippe Muray, *Le XIXe siècle à travers les âges* (Paris, 1999).
47 In this context, see Eric Blondel, *Nietzsche, the Body and Culture:
   Philosophy as a Philological Genealogy*, trans. Seán Hand
   (Stanford, CA, 1991), who explores the interrelationship between
   Nietzschean 'cynicism' (in the ancient, philosophical sense) and
   positive fact (as understood in modern science and medicine).
48 Friedrich Nietzsche, *The Gay Science: With a Prelude in Rhymes
   and an Appendix of Songs*, trans. Walter Kaufmann (New York,
   1974), p. 181.
49 For apposite discussion, especially in relation to modernist
   aesthetics, see David Pan, *Primitive Renaissance: Rethinking
   German Expressionism* (Lincoln, NE, 2001), pp. 29–82.
50 Ernst Bertram, *Nietzsche: Attempt at a Mythology*, trans. Robert
   E. Norton (Champaign, IL, 2009), p. 128.
51 Significantly, this title – which Nietzsche proudly adopted – is
   the same one Doctor Torty applies to himself in 'Happiness in
   Crime' (Barbey d'Aurevilly, *Diaboliques*, p. 120).

7 The Godawful Truth

 1 Joseph de Maistre, *Saint Petersburg Dialogues; or, Conversations
   on the Temporal Government of Providence*, trans. Richard A.
   Lebrun (Kingston, ON, 1993), p. 215.
 2 Ibid., p. 214.
 3 Ibid., p. 216.

4 Ibid., p. 211.

5 Peter Gay, *Modernism: The Lure of Heresy from Baudelaire to Beckett and Beyond* (New York, 2008), p. 4.

6 Françoise Meltzer, *Seeing Double: Baudelaire's Modernity* (Chicago, IL, 2011), pp. 30–57.

7 James Joyce, *Ulysses* (New York, 1986), p. 411 (chapter 15, ll. 2,097–8).

8 Gay, *Modernism*, p. 4.

9 See Chapter Five.

10 See Anna Balakian, *Surrealism: The Road to the Absolute* (Chicago, IL, 1986), pp. 50–66.

11 Comte de Lautréamont, *Maldoror and the Complete Works*, trans. Alexis Lykiard (Boston, MA, 1994), pp. 76–7.

12 Ibid., p. 77.

13 Ibid., p. 27.

14 See Robert Faurisson, *A-t-on lu Lautréamont?* (Paris, 1972).

15 Charles Baudelaire, *Selected Writings on Art and Artists*, trans. P. E. Charvet (Cambridge, 1972), p. 148.

16 Quoted in Peter D. G. Brown, *Oskar Panizza: His Life and Works* (New York, 1983), p. 9; biographical information is taken from this book.

17 Peter D. G. Brown, *Oskar Panizza and 'The Love Council': A History of the Scandalous Play on Stage and in Court, with the Complete Text in English and a Biography of the Author* (Jefferson, NC, 2010).

18 Oskar Panizza, *The Pig: In Poetic, Mythological, and Moral-historical Perspective*, trans. Erik Butler (Cambridge, MA, 2016), p. 4.

19 See Peter Gay, *A Godless Jew: Freud, Atheism, and the Making of Psychoanalysis* (New Haven, CT, 1987).

20 This view goes back to the pioneering work of German sociologist Max Weber (1864–1920); see *The Protestant Ethic and the 'Spirit' of Capitalism and Other Writings*, trans. Peter Baehr (New York, 2002).

21 Friedrich Nietzsche, *Beyond Good and Evil: Prelude to a Philosophy of the Future*, trans. Judith Norman (Cambridge, 2002), p. 38.

22 For a nuanced account with details and appropriate caveats, see Jonathan Israel, *Radical Enlightenment: Philosophy and the Making of Modernity, 1650–1750* (Oxford, 2002).

23 See Matthew 12:46–50: 'While he yet talked to the people, behold, his mother and his brethren stood without, desiring to speak with him. Then one said unto him, "Behold, thy mother and thy brethren stand without, desiring to speak with thee." But he answered and said unto him that told him, "Who is my mother? And who are my brethren?" And he stretched forth his hand toward his disciples, and said, "Behold my mother and my brethren! For whosoever shall do the will of my Father which is in heaven, the same is my brother, and sister, and mother."'

24 John Haldon, *Warfare, State and Society in the Byzantine World, 565–1204* (London, 1999), pp. 23–4.

25 Ernst Jünger, *Storm of Steel*, trans. Michael Hofmann (New York, 2004), p. 5.

26 See, for example, Enzo Traverso, *Fire and Blood: The European Civil War, 1914–1945*, trans. David Fernbach (London, 2016).

27 See Frank Kermode, *The Sense of an Ending: Studies in the Theory of Fiction* (Oxford, 2000), especially pp. 93–126.

28 William Butler Yeats, *The Collected Poems of William Butler Yeats* (Ware, Hertfordshire, 2000), p. 158.

29 Yuri Slezkine, *The House of Government: A Saga of the Russian Revolution* (Princeton, NJ, 2017), p. 23; the next two quotes are taken from the same page.

30 See Andrew Baruch Wachtel and Ilya Vinitsky, *Russian Literature* (Cambridge, 2009), particularly pp. 158–203.

31 Fyodor Dostoevsky, *Notes from Underground*, trans. Richard Pevear and Larissa Volokhonsky (New York, 1994), pp. 25–6.

32 Fyodor Dostoevsky, *Demons: A Novel in Three Parts*, trans. Richard Pevear and Larissa Volokhonsky (New York, 1995), p. 33.

33 See Arthur O. Lovejoy, *The Great Chain of Being: A Study of the History of an Idea* (Cambridge, MA, 1964).

34 Daniel C. Dennett, *Darwin's Dangerous Idea: Evolution and the Meaning of Life* (New York, 1995), especially pp. 64–8.

35 Michel Foucault, *The History of Sexuality*, vol. I: *An Introduction*, trans. Robert Hurley (New York, 1978), p. 146.

36 Ibid.

37 Gian Pietro Lucini, *Revolverate e Nuove revolverate*, ed. Edoardo Sanguineti (Turin, 1975), pp. 168–9.

38 Ibid., p. 169.

39 Ibid.
40 Ibid., p. 170.
41 Ibid., p. 183; the quote in the next sentence comes from the same page.
42 Ibid., p. 188.
43 See Chapter Two.
44 Gertrude Stein, *Gertrude Stein's America*, ed. Gilbert A. Harrison (New York, 1996), p. 90.
45 See Kimberly Jannarone, *Artaud and His Doubles* (Ann Arbor, MI, 2012).
46 Gottfried Benn, 'Urgesicht', in *Gesammelte Werke*, 4 vols, ed. Dieter Wellershoff (Stuttgart, 1978), vol. II, p. 107; the next two quotes are from the same page. Readers may wish to compare the translation published in Gottfried Benn, *Primal Vision: Selected Writings of Gottfried Benn*, ed. E. B. Ashton (New York, 1971), pp. 29–38.
47 Ibid., p. 115.
48 T. S. Eliot, *Collected Poems, 1909–1962* (New York, 1991), p. 82.
49 Benn, 'Urgesicht', p. 117.
50 Ibid.
51 Ibid., p. 118.
52 C. S. Lewis, *The C. S. Lewis Signature Classics* (New York, 2017), p. 206; quotes below are from the same page and p. 250.

8 A Satanic Symphony

1 'Sorrow shall take hold on the inhabitants of Palestina . . . Fear and dread shall fall upon them; by the greatness of thine arm they shall be as still as a stone . . . Thou shalt bring [thy people] in, and plant them in the mountain of thine inheritance, in the place, O Lord, which thou hast made for thee to dwell in' (Exodus 15:14–17).
2 Augustine, *Confessions*, p. 211.
3 Ibid., p. 207.
4 Ibid., pp. 123–4, 267.
5 Kevin Madigan, *Medieval Christianity: A New History* (New Haven, CT, 2015), pp. 419–22.
6 Hildegard of Bingen, *Ordo Virtutum*, in *Nine Medieval Plays*, ed. Peter Dronke (Cambridge, 1994), p. 165 [l. 59 of the Latin].
7 Ibid., p. 179 [ll. 229–34].

8 See Chapter One.

9 See Chapter Three.

10 Hildegard of Bingen, *Ordo Virtutum*, p. 164 [l. 59].

11 Ibid., p. 179 [ll. 247–51].

12 Plato, *The Republic*, trans. Allan Bloom (New York, 1991), especially p. 54 and pp. 82–91; the translator's introduction provides apposite commentary, as well.

13 Dante, *Paradiso*, I, 76–84.

14 Dante, *Inferno*, XXI, 139.

15 Quoted in Dietrich Bartel, *Musica Poetica: Musical-rhetorical Figures in German Baroque Music* (Lincoln, NE, 1997), p. 6.

16 Ibid., pp. 4–5.

17 Ibid., p. 7.

18 Ibid., p. 6.

19 Carlos M. N. Eire, *Reformations: The Early Modern World, 1450–1650* (New Haven, CT, 2016), p. 185.

20 Wilbur F. Tillett DD, ed., *Our Hymns and Their Authors: An Annotated Edition of the Hymn Book* (Nashville, TN, 1892), p. 220; translated by Frederick H. Hedge.

21 Luther switches the polarity from defence to offence inasmuch as God 'hath willed / His truth to triumph through us'. 'Christ Jesus' appears in a martial light, as 'Lord Sabaoth'; in Hebrew, this title means 'Lord of the Hosts' – in other words, a commander of armies, not the Prince of Peace who turns the other cheek.

22 Quotations follow John Milton, *Complete Poems and Major Prose*, ed. Merritt Y. Hughes (New York, 1957), pp. 89–114, by line number; here: *Comus*, 571.

23 Ibid., 278, 186.

24 Ibid., 187.

25 Ibid., 304, 571.

26 Ibid., unnumbered (between ll. 658 and 659).

27 Ibid., 907, 904.

28 Ibid., 278.

29 Darren Oldridge, *The Devil in Tudor and Stuart England* (Stroud, 2010), p. 38.

30 Milton, *Comus*, 415, 436–7.

31 Ibid., 916–17.

32 Ibid., unnumbered (between ll. 92 and 93).

33 Ibid., 91–2.

34 Thrysabulos Georgiades, *Music and Language: The Rise of Western Music as Exemplified in Settings of the Mass*, trans. Marie Louise Göllner (Cambridge, 1982), pp. 103–4.

35 Schoenberg was hardly thrilled. See Hermann Kurzke, *Thomas Mann: Life as a Work of Art*, trans. Leslie Wilson (Princeton, NJ, 2002), pp. 477–9.

36 Oswald Spengler, *The Decline of the West*, abridged edition, trans. Charles Francis Atkinson (Oxford, 1991), p. xxxi.

37 Ibid., p. 197.

38 Thomas Mann, *Doctor Faustus: The Life of the German Composer Adrian Leverkuhn as Told by a Friend*, trans. John E. Woods (New York, 1999), p. 257.

39 Ibid., pp. 230, 242, 259.

40 Ibid., p. 253.

41 Ibid., p. 254.

42 Ibid., p. 252.

43 Ibid., pp. 258–9.

44 See Chapter Seven.

45 Theodor W. Adorno, 'On Popular Music', in *Essays on Music*, ed. Richard Leppert (Berkeley, CA, 2002), p. 438.

46 *The Decline of Western Civilization*, as two documentaries (now some forty years old) by Penelope Spheeris put it with cheery abandon.

Coda

1 Quoted (here and below) in Frank Lentricchia and Jody McAuliffe, *Crimes of Art and Terror* (Chicago, IL, 2003), pp. 6–7.

2 Theodor Adorno, *Minima Moralia: Reflections on a Damaged Life*, trans. E.F.N. Jephcott (London, 2005), p. 111.

3 Georg Wilhelm Friedrich Hegel, *Lectures on the Philosophy of World History: Introduction*, trans. H. B. Nisbet (Cambridge, 1984), pp. 68–9.

4 See for example, Michael Moynihan and Didrik Soderlind, *Lords of Chaos: The Bloody Rise of the Satanic Metal Underground* (Los Angeles, CA, 1998).

5 See Per Faxneld and Jesper Aa. Petersen, eds, *The Devil's Party: Satanism In Modernity* (Oxford, 2012), especially pp. 167–88.

SELECT BIBLIOGRAPHY

Almond, Philip C., *The Devil: A New Biography* (Ithaca, NY, 2014)

Alter, Robert, ed. and trans., *The Wisdom Books: Job, Proverbs, and Ecclesiastes: A Translation with Commentary* (New York, 2011)

Boyd, Gregory A., *Satan and the Problem of Evil: Constructing a Trinitarian Warfare Theodicy* (London, 2001)

Carus, Paul, *The History of the Devil and the Idea of Evil: From the Earliest Times to the Present Day* (Chicago, IL, 1900)

Charlesworth, James H., *The Good and Evil Serpent: How a Universal Symbol Became Christianized* (New Haven, CT, 2010)

Cohn, Norman, *Europe's Inner Demons: An Enquiry Inspired by the Great Witch-hunt* (New York, 1975)

De La Torre, Miguel, and Albert Hernandez, *The Quest for the Historical Satan* (Minneapolis, MN, 2011)

Dyrendal, Asbjorn, James R. Lewis and Jesper Aa. Petersen, *The Invention of Satanism* (Oxford, 2015)

Faxneld, Per, and Jesper Aa. Petersen, eds, *The Devil's Party: Satanism in Modernity* (Oxford, 2012)

Flusser, Vilém, *The History of the Devil*, trans. Rodrigo Maltez Novaes (Minneapolis, MN, 2014)

Forsyth, Neil, *The Old Enemy: Satan and the Combat Myth* (Princeton, NJ, 1987)

—, *The Satanic Epic* (Princeton, NJ, 2003)

Harkins, Angela Kim, Kelley Coblentz Bautch and John C. Endres, eds, *The Watchers in Jewish and Christian Traditions* (Minneapolis, MN, 2014)

Kelly, Henry Ansgar, *Satan: A Biography* (Cambridge, 2006)

—, *Satan in the Bible: God's Minister of Justice* (Eugene, OR, 2017)

Le Goff, Jacques, *The Birth of Purgatory* (Chicago, IL, 1986)

Levack, Brian P., *The Witch-hunt in Early Modern Europe* (London, 2006)

Messadié, Gerald, *A History of the Devil*, trans. Marc Romano (New York, 1996)

Moore, R. I., *The Formation of a Persecuting Society: Authority and Deviance in Western Europe, 950–1250* (Oxford, 2007)

—, *The War on Heresy* (Cambridge, MA, 2014)

Muchembled, Robert, *A History of the Devil: From the Middle Ages to the Present*, trans. Jean Birrell (Oxford, 2003)

Oldridge, Darren. *The Devil in Tudor and Stuart England* (Stroud, 2010)

—, *The Devil: A Very Short Introduction* (Oxford, 2012)

Pagels, Elaine, *The Gnostic Gospels* (New York, 1989)

—, *The Origin of Satan: How Christians Demonized Jews, Pagans, and Heretics* (New York, 1996)

—, *Revelations: Visions, Prophecy, and Politics in the Book of Revelation* (New York, 2013)

Palmer, Philip Mason, and Robert Pattison More, *The Sources of the Faust Tradition: From Simon Magus to Lessing* (Oxford, 1936)

Poole, W. Scott, *Satan in America: The Devil We Know* (Lanham, MD, 2010)

Russell, Jeffrey Burton, *Lucifer: The Devil in the Middle Ages* (Ithaca, NY, 1984)

—, *Witchcraft in the Middle Ages* (Ithaca, NY, 1984)

—, *Satan: The Early Christian Tradition* (Ithaca, NY, 1987)

Stokes, Ryan E., *The Satan: How God's Executioner Became the Enemy* (Grand Rapids, MI, 2019)

Stuckenbruck, Loren, *The Myth of Rebellious Angels: Studies in Second Temple Judaism and New Testament Texts* (Grand Rapids, MI, 2014)

Trachtenberg, Joshua, *The Devil and the Jews: The Medieval Conception of the Jew and Its Relation to Modern Anti-semitism* (Lincoln, NE, 2002)

Trevor-Roper, H. R., *The European Witch-craze of the Sixteenth and Seventeenth Centuries, and Other Essays* (New York, 1969)

Walton, John H., and J. Harvey Walton, *Demons and Spirits in Biblical Theology: Reading the Biblical Text in Its Cultural and Literary Context* (Eugene, OR, 2019)

Wray, T. J., and Gregory Mobley, *The Birth of Satan: Tracing the Devil's Biblical Roots* (New York, 2005)

ACKNOWLEDGEMENTS

Thanks to friends and family, especially Anneliese, and the cats. The human beings offered criticism and suggestions; the quadrupeds volunteered emotional support (at least by my understanding). To Kimberly I owe an unpayable debt for almost half a lifetime of companionship – and all the well-spent years of earthly existence. Her willingness to read drafts and ideas for righting wayward strains of argument gave the book substance where otherwise ghostly figments would clank and howl. Finally, thanks to Alex Ciobanu, Michael Leaman and Amy Salter at Reaktion Books for their patience and help as the project took form and materialized in the volume at hand.

PHOTO ACKNOWLEDGEMENTS

The author and publishers wish to express their thanks to the below sources of illustrative material and/or permission to reproduce it. Some locations of artworks are also given below, in the interest of brevity:

Albright-Knox Art Gallery, Buffalo, NY: p. 230; Alte Pinakothek, Munich: p. 6; from J. Barbey d'Aurevilly, *Les Diaboliques* (Paris, 1886): p. 148; Beinecke Rare Book & Manuscript Library, Yale University, New Haven, CT: p. 75; from Gottfried Benn, *Morgue und andere Gedichte* (Munich, 1923), photo courtesy Hornbake Library, University of Maryland, College Park, MD: p. 193; Bibliothèque nationale de France, Paris: p. 217; from Pierre-Jules Hetzel, pseud. P.-J. Stahl, ed., *Le Diable à Paris: Paris et les Parisiens* (Paris, 1845): p. 139; from Pierre-Jules Hetzel, pseud. P.-J. Stahl, ed., *Scènes de la vie privée et publique des animaux*, vol. I (Paris, 1842), photo courtesy Getty Research Institute, Los Angeles: p. 188; The J. Paul Getty Museum, Los Angeles: pp. 48, 165; The Metropolitan Museum of Art, New York: pp. 81, 98, 117; The Morgan Library & Museum, New York/photo courtesy The Morgan Library & Museum: p. 86; Open Access Image from the Davison Art Center, Wesleyan University, Middletown, CT (photo: R. Lee): p. 31; Rijksmuseum, Amsterdam: pp. 16, 53, 112, 126, 132, 135, 175, 222, 226; Schloss Friedenstein, Gotha/photo Minneapolis Institute of Arts, MN: p. 208; from Robert Vaughan, ed., *Milton's Paradise Lost, Illustrated by Gustave Doré, Edited with Notes and a Life of Milton* (London and New York, 1866): p. 123.

Richard Mortel, the copyright holder of the image on p. 71, has published it online under conditions imposed by a Creative Commons

Attribution 2.0 Generic License. Wellcome Collection, the copyright holder of the images on p. 62, has published it online under conditions imposed by a Creative Commons Attribution 4.0 International License.

Readers are free to:

share – copy and redistribute the material in any medium or format.

adapt – remix, transform, and build upon the material for any purpose, even commercially.

Under the following terms:

attribution – You must give appropriate credit, provide a link to the license, and indicate if changes were made. You may do so in any reasonable manner, but not in any way that suggests the licensor endorses you or your use.

share alike – If you remix, transform, or build upon the material, you must distribute your contributions under the same license as the original.

INDEX

Page numbers in *italics* refer to illustrations